# MASTERING
## THE POWER OF YOUR
# EMOTIONS

HOW TO CONTROL WHAT HAPPENS IN YOU
IRRESPECTIVE OF WHAT HAPPENS TO YOU

(4th Edition)

Elisha O. Ogbonna

**Mastering the Power of Your Emotions** by Elisha O. Ogbonna
This book is written to provide information and motivation to readers. Its purpose is not to render any type of psychological, legal, or professional advice of any kind. The content is the sole opinion and expression of the author, and not necessarily that of the publisher.

Copyright © 2021 by Elisha O. Ogbonna

All rights reserved.
No part of this publication may be reproduced in any form, or by any means, electronic or mechanical, including photocopying, recording, or any information browsing, storage, or retrieval system, without permission in writing from the Author.

*Most of the stories presented within this book are from media sources and do not originate from me (the author). I have made every effort to ensure that the information within this book was correct at the time it was extracted from their primary sources. In any situation where any of the stories differs from those available in various sources, official prints and update posts of source sites take precedence. I do not assume and hereby disclaims any liability to party for any new changes, update, new development, errors or omission, whether such errors or omissions result from accident, negligence, or any other cause.*

Scripture quotations marked KJV are taken from the King James Version of the Bible, which is in the public domain. Scripture quotations marked NIV are taken from the Holy Bible, NEW INTERNATIONAL VERSION®. Copyright © 1973, 1978, 1984, 2011 by Biblica, Inc.

ISBN
978-1-7772771-9-2 (Hardcover)
978-1-7772771-8-5 (Paperback)
978-1-7777461-0-0 (eBook)
978-1-7777461-1-7 (audio)

1. Self-Help, Emotions
2. Self-Help, Mood Disorders, Depression
3. Self-help, Personal Growth, Self-Esteem

Published by
Prinoelio Press, Ontario, Canada
For: https://www.elishaogbonna.com

# Dedication

my late parents,
Mr. & Mrs. Ogbonna Nwobodo,

and

To those who are hurting and
seek to be free from emotional trauma.

# TABLE OF CONTENTS

**DEDICATION**                             V

**INTRODUCTION**              1

**CHAPTER ONE**

The Five Most Distressing Emotions ................................................................. 5

**CHAPTER TWO:**

The Relativity and Reality of Emotions ............................................................ 43

**CHAPTER THREE:**

Sources of Emotional Distress ........................................................................ 57

**CHAPTER FOUR:**

Levels of Emotional Crisis ............................................................................... 87

**CHAPTER FIVE:**

The Five Laws of Emotions ........................................................................... 101

**CHAPTER SIX:**

The Grip of Depression ................................................................................. 117

**CHAPTER SEVEN:**

The Torment of Guilt and Shame ................................................................. 135

## CHAPTER EIGHT:

The Agony of Abandonment ........................................................................ 145

## CHAPTER NINE:

The Deceptions of Suicidal Thoughts ............................................................ 155

## CHAPTER TEN:

Overcoming Self-complexes......................................................................... 171

## CHAPTER ELEVEN:

Guide for Handling Problem Emotions ......................................................... 191

## CHAPTER TWELVE:

Anonymous Threats: Emotional Risk and Safe Haven .................................. 201

## CHAPTER THIRTEEN:

Releasing Negative Emotions....................................................................... 213

## TAKING STOCK OF YOUR EMOTIONAL HEALTH    223

## BIBLIOGRAPHY    239

# Introduction

A couple of years ago, we moved from Guelph to Kitchener, Ontario, so that my wife could study at the Kitchener campus of Conestoga College. We sat down as a family to consider the impact it would have on family activities before making any decision and figured out how to make the move less stressful.

There were many positive reasons for the move except finding a job in Kitchener for myself and transportation for the family. My wife wanted more flexibility and to be able to use public transit when necessary for her commute to and from school. To minimize stress and maximize time for family activities, my wife wanted to be able to get home early without having to drive long distances or being stuck in traffic for long periods of time. So, we decided to find accommodation relatively close to her campus.

I also wanted the flexibility to be able to use the car within the municipality or ride the Grand River Transit (GRT), the public transport operator for the tri-city area of Kitchener, Waterloo, and Cambridge. As part of my job search, I applied to postings in the tri-city area. I also went to various recruiting agencies for interviews and to submit my resume. Within weeks, I was successful at finding a job through Pivotal Integrated HR Solutions. The employer was located in Cambridge, which is about twenty-one kilometers from Kitchener. This was ideal for me in terms of managing local transportation to and from work.

After a few months in my new position, I had scored some solid points for my effectiveness and efficiency. Overall, I liked the position, and my supervisor was happy with me. The employees were one big productive team. My family was happy with our new life as well, and everything was good at home and work until a certain day.

On that day, I was assigned to load parts onto a conveyor belt with a colleague named Tyler. As I began my work, something unexpected happened. Tyler walked up to me and stood in my way. He grabbed the automotive part that I had been assigned to load from my hand, hung that part, and walked back to the bin to get another part that I was responsible for putting on the conveyor. We didn't exchange a word, and I stood still in confusion.

When I finally observed the look on his face, I knew that he must be struggling with something. I moved to his station, and because I knew how to do his job, I started to do it. It was as if we had intentionally decided to swap stations. I wanted to avoid all the feelings, chaos, and pressure that are ultimately intertwined with workplace drama. I worked at his station for about an hour, and then Tyler moved back and started doing the very job he should have been doing from the beginning. In response, I walked back to my original station and continued working on my assigned duties.

Halfway into our shift, without asking, Tyler went to the storage room and got a pair of gloves and handed them over to me. A few minutes later, he walked up to me and said, "I am sorry, man, if I got in your way." I told him there was no problem. He remained at his station for the rest of the shift and didn't come over to my station again. I didn't ask him if I had done anything wrong, as I knew I hadn't.

The following day, his countenance had improved, he was talking to people, and he appeared a little more relaxed. I waited until the right time to ask him the reason for his actions on the previous day. It was then that he told me he had quarreled with his girlfriend before coming to work, and she had left him without saying if she was going to come back.

What I observed with Tyler is something that can happen to all of us. Events in our lives often influence our thinking, impact our mood, and affect our actions. Like a hungry lion seeking out a prey, the feelings caused by these events thrust out claws and hurt us deeply. These feelings push us to extremes—either hot or cold. If we are hot, we become furious and boil uncontrollably, but if we are cold, we withdraw, make excuses, complain, or blame or sabotage other people.
Time and time again, I have heard people say, "It is the way I am; there's nothing I can do about it" or "I am hot tempered" or "I am shy, and I don't think I can speak in public" or "I am afraid of the future." The list keeps going.

The truth is, everyone has feelings. Everyone has, at one point or another, cried in pain. Likewise, we have experienced anger and fear at one point. There are no exceptions to this fact. As long as we go to work, meet people, have relationships, or even stay at home by ourselves, we will experience a myriad of feelings every day in our lives.

Emotion is the feeling portion of our being. It is the central and most important part of our life next to our mind. Our feelings are influenced either from inward events (in our mind) or outward events (from our physical surroundings). Emotions are the responses we produce when we experience complex situations in life. They represent the internal descriptions we give to these events and empower the will for action. Emotion gives life and action to our thoughts.

Emotion is connected to mood and disposition, as well as to our personality and character. It cannot be separated from our reactions. Our emotions are a result of our perceptions, interpretations, and understanding of events. For example, when we are angry, it reveals that we feel hurt by an event, whereas when we are joyful, it suggests that we regard a situation as pleasant.

Are you hurting? Are you in pain from betrayal, depression, or anger? Has someone you love deserted you? Do you want to conquer the enemy called fear? Do you have low self-esteem? Do you want to know how to keep and protect your relationships? Are you easily irritated when dealing with people? Are you stressed out or frustrated? Do you feel like taking your life because of what you are going through right now?

Save yourself from living a miserable life. This book is the tool you need to develop control and be in charge of your life. Stop allowing other people's words and actions to determine how you operate in life. Learn the skills you need to keep control of your emotions regardless of the situations you face.

This book is for everyone who wants to heal from pain and bitterness. It is for those who want to have a successful and happy life, and it is for those who want to make their own decisions and not have life's events decided for them by others or their own circumstances. This book is for those who want to develop good self-esteem, attain freedom, and become the master of their emotions.

# Chapter One
## The Five Most Distressing Emotions

Every one of us is emotionally wired to be happy or sad. Our individual desires move us to pursue things that we believe will give us pleasure or joy. Everything we do in this life is either influenced by our emotions or will. The pursuit of happiness and satisfaction is everyone's goal. This is evident when we move from one city to another, one job to another or one career to another. It is all about happiness and fulfillment. Whatever we have acquired or look forward to acquiring—house, furniture, car, education, or business success—is connected to our desires. We work hard and make smart decisions to get what we believe will meet our needs, goals, desires, and dreams.

What is the bottom line for all our toil and labor under the sun? It is in my opinion to be happy and find some level of satisfaction. When we achieve our goals, we are happy, and with good feeling from our accomplishment, we are often motivated to accomplish more. Positive emotions—enthusiasm, anticipation, hope, or joy—are uplifting and charming. We love and want them. We love it when things are going well on our terms. It is true for every human.

However, emotions are like day and night and the seasons of nature. Daytime comes and makes way for the night at sunset. Likewise, nighttime makes way for the day at dawn. Regardless of how much we love summer, when the time comes, winter must show up.

Similarly, positive emotions are good, and we desire to hold on to them with a tight fist, but the time usually comes when they disappear. They disappear when we face challenges, meet obstacles, or are rejected. While it is great not to experience rejection, failure, or loss, it is impossible to escape them as long as we are alive, have family, or meet people. The ups and downs of life are inevitable. At one point or another, they will definitely find their way into our life to stir our emotions for actions.

When our desire hits a roadblock, we may experience anger. When we believe something negative is going to happen, we are likely to experience fear. Whereas most negative emotions are not bad but when they remain active their effects can be distressing. Distressing emotions can be damaging when their energies are not harnessed properly. This is especially true when we are distressed and one of these damaging negative emotions steer us into destructive actions. Such negative emotions can be powerful enough to compel and propel us to make choices that could hurt ourselves or someone else.

Fear, anger, hatred, jealousy, and grief are the top five most distressing emotions. It is important that we gain a thorough understanding of how to master them in order to protect and grow our relationships at home, work, and in our community. We cannot wish negative feelings away by assuming that there is nothing we can do about our feelings. If we do, we hand our life and destiny over to feelings that would ultimately ruin them. The good news is that while we cannot control how we feel, we can control what we do, regardless of how bad we feel. Also, we can reduce or eliminate the impact of negative feelings regardless of the height or breadth of their influence. We can achieve more, develop great interpersonal skills, and ultimately carry out our daily duties with a heart free of hate and bitterness. The following are the five most distressing emotions everyone should watch out for.

## Fear

Fear is the feeling of anxiety and agitation caused by the presence or imminence of danger. It is the feeling of disquiet and/or apprehension that causes a person to dread or be uneasy about what will happen next. Other words that could be used to describe fear are panic, terror, horror, alarm, dismay, fright, dread, and so on.

Fear is distressing and is associated with feeling alarmed, which may be for real or imaginary reasons. When we feel threatened by imminent danger, we become uneasy until our sense of security is restored.

The only healthy form of fear is a reverential awe, such as the one that a person might feel for God. Otherwise, fear in every other sense is a destroyer.

Many fears come naturally, and it is common to be afraid of things that we perceive as threatening or dangerous. From birth to adulthood, human life is characterized by fear every step of the way. For example, a newborn baby has two instinctive fears: the fear of falling and the fear of loud noises. When young children hold on to their parents' clothing and refuse to let go, they are displaying that they feel safer with their parents. In their young minds, they are afraid of the unfamiliar and what could possibly hurt them.

When parents play with their toddlers and encourage them to walk on their own, children sometimes sit down in fear. But as soon as they become aware that there is support and that their parents will protect them from falling, they gain the confidence to keep trying. In order for toddlers to learn to walk, they must conquer the fear of falling. They achieve this through confidence and practice.

Loud noises are the second instinctive fear experienced by babies. It makes them uneasy and uncomfortable. They experience shock and sometimes will begin to cry. This is the way that babies, toddlers, and young children reveal their feelings of fear. As they grow up and begin to see and understand the sources of the noise, their perceptions change, and they become less fearful.

For adults, there are seven fundamental fears that we usually face at least once in our lives, and sometimes even every day. They include fear of criticism, fear of rejection,[1] fear of loss (either of a loved one or the things we love most), fear of poverty, fear of sickness, fear of old age, and fear of death.

When fear is at work in our life, it enslaves us by blinding us to opportunities that surround us. It directs all our attention and thinking towards failure. Every opportunity that comes by will, in our perception, can be seen as a potential pitfall because it makes us dwell on the past failures.

Fear is a dangerous and devastating emotion. It is the complete opposite of faith. If faith can facilitate the healing of the sick, fear can gradually take them on a journey to their grave. People of great faith do great things, and people with great fear achieve nothing in life. One the one hand, faith makes people great, while on the other hand, fear makes people inadequate. Fear can torment the human spirit, soul, and body. Fear also gives birth to anxiety, and anxiety kills. Fear does not care about one's age or status. It is the destroyer of destiny. It can make the strongest humans become the weakest.

When you overcome fear, new facts emerge because your spirit will grow. Just like a baby who has conquered the fear of falling when they took the risk to stand and walk, we can also conquer our fears by

---

[1] These are explored further in Chapter 3

taking risks, thereby making it easier to get rid of similar fears in the future and becoming even stronger to face greater fears. Risk is what human nature hates, but where we are today is the product of risk. Everything around us that science and technology has achieved are products of risk. The biological research that gives birth to vaccines, pills, and other medical treatments is in one way or the other a result of risk. We often dread taking a risk, but when we don't take risks, we fail. We need to conquer our fears to succeed in life. To conquer fear, we must all operate with the principle of faith—that is, we must believe and trust that something good will happen regardless of the threatening circumstances.

The key to managing our fears is to understand what we are afraid of and why we are afraid of it, and to explore available options to achieve what we want. Some of the options may be to persevere or retreat, but not to surrender. When we take a moment to pause and think about our fears, we often begin to see solutions to our problems. For example, I remembered that at my current workplace, I was late for the interview while I had planned to be a least thirty minutes early. My wife took my car and went for shopping. When she came back, I had already lost fifteen minutes of the planned schedule, but that was not too bad. I met heavy traffic on the way and the traffic jam caused me to be late for my job interview. I was filled with fear that I would lose that job opportunity.

My emotions were running high, and I was thrown into deep confusion. While sitting in the car at a traffic signal, I remembered that I had two options. First option was to turn back and go home, and the second option was to drive to the company and apologize to the interviewer for being late. I chose the second option and by choosing that option, I persevered and chose to face my fear. Then came the light, and like a flash it said, "Call the receptionist." I called and told the receptionist about the situation and that I will be ten to fifteen minutes late for the interview. The receptionist told me that she would pass the information to the interviewer.

Upon arrival at the company, I met with the receptionist and explained to her the whole situation. She called the interviewers and let them know that I had arrived. They came over, and I repeated the same thing what I'd told the receptionist on phone. They confirmed getting my message and would proceed with the interview. I had the interview and got hired. I am in no way promoting lateness, but this example serves as a lesson for anyone who feels knocked down by the unforeseen circumstances and has been filled with fear that the worst would happen. Pick yourself up from where you have fallen, encourage yourself, and try again. Keep the motion on, and it will let fears and anxiety get out of your way.

There is no reason for fear and you just need to take a step. Success and failure, riches and poverty, health and sickness, acceptance and rejection, and even life and death are two roads that goes in different directions. If you want one, you must refuse the other. You cannot be going in both directions at the same time. It is your duty to know what you want in life, and identify the road that will take you there.

When it comes to the fear of death, I would advise that we should take the example of ant's life. In case you feel a lesson from ants is not comparable, let us consider the life of a farmer. Farming is the activity of growing crops and or raising livestock, that holds great lesson for us. The various steps for growing crops include loosening the soil, seeding, special watering, transplanting, and harvesting, among others. All these activities are carried out in good faith. Farmers should not worry about the harvest, but they carry out their farming activities as required. They spend time and resources to follow all steps of agricultural practices, including preparation of soil, sowing, adding manure and fertilizers, and irrigation. Once the crop is ready and it is time for harvesting, they perform harvesting and store the crop. And after harvest, some crops may be stored for themselves and the remaining is sold to the traders.

Do farmers worry about losing all their crops due to drought, flood, birds, or pests? Does it stop them from farming? Of course, not! Why would you worry about the unknown? Why would you terrorize yourself with something that may never happen soon? Why die before the actual death? The fear of death cannot change human beings' destiny. It rather keeps its victims dying and may claim their lives before time. It is not a solution, but remains a problem. Farmers do not declare drought or famine before they actually happen. They are mostly optimistic, even when the weather does not look favourable.

Optimism keeps farmers and dreamers going. They persevere even in the midst of the storm. You can look at the bright side of life and worry less about the unsure future. Let go of the worry about something that everyone will have to experience at some point in their life. You are full of life, and you have a bright future. You need to saturate your mind daily with possibility and positivity. If you believe negative things will only happen, why not believe that the positive things can also happen instead? What people believe often comes their way. Consciously, flood your heart with the expectation of great things—even amid negative occurrences— and it will amaze you how the good things in life will flow to you. This is one of the best ways to defeat fear—believe in positive outcomes. Even if you have a chronic disease, the stronger your faith is, the more certain it is that you will get well. Fear respects faith as darkness respects light.

In the analysis regarding the ultimate fear—fear of death—certain facts emerge. There are three main elements in the fear of death. The first is the fear of the physical process of dying. This may be horrifying for some people, yet, for many in today's world, there is the consolation of knowing that pain-killing drugs can dull the edge of the most excruciating pain. The second element of this is the fear of extinction—the dreadful thought that death is indeed the end of everything, including our loves and hopes. The third element in the fear of death is the fear of judgement. This fear is not as strong as it once was, since fewer people attend church and today fewer sermons are preached on the topic of judgement. Yet a fear of judgement resides in one's conscience, even though some people are in denial of it. It finds support in the iron law of cause and effect. Many religious and non-religious folks acknowledge that the actions people take have a way of coming back to haunt them.

Someone who feels overwhelmed by the fear of extinction or the fear of judgement needs reassurance. They need the conviction that even though life experiences are not the same for all, the common denominator is that the end will come with justice. The fear of extinction has been debunked by the testimonies that people who died and were revived back to life. The testimonies in the Holy Book attest to the fact that death is not the end of everything. Death is ultimately a transition—a transition from the material world to the spiritual world. It is beyond science, because science deals with matter (material things). Even though, some people can choose to argue that death is the end of all things. And those who do should consider what happens in night dreams and the concept of paranormal activities that many religions believe and experience. The concept of a human soul and some spiritual experiences are the proof of that death is not the end of life, but the beginning of supernatural living.

If you belong to the group of people imprisoned in the fear of judgement, I will encourage you to live a good life. The concept of purity is living a life without any immoral or wicked behaviour. People who choose the pathway of love and peace live without fear of condemnation. If we can choose the path of love, forgiveness, and giving, we can rest assured that judgement would be to our misfortune. In the revealed biblical truth, the commandment is to love God and people. A step further, the biblical recommendation for the outright fix for the fear of judgement is to believe in Jesus, who will judge the world of their sins on the last day. Believing in Jesus Christ, the Bible says, is the guarantee for everlasting life [paraphrased].[2]

## Anger

Anger is a strong feeling of displeasure or hostility. It is a feeling of great annoyance or antagonism because of some real or supposed grievance. It is a violent and bitter feeling against someone or something and is often accompanied by a desire to "get even" with the cause of the pain or discomfort.

Like desire, anger can exist as a "neutral" emotion. It is what you add to it that makes it good or bad. What matters is what you do with it. Like with anything else, you can use it to build or to destroy. Anger is only justified when it is directed to finding solutions to problems. It should not take control of you or make you do what you do not want to do.

Anger is a destructive emotion if it is not properly managed. It can eat into the fabric of one's spirit, soul, and body. Anger can ruin your life, your health and destroy your normal bodily functions. Anger if carried for a long time, can create headaches, restlessness, confusion, and other forms of internal maladies. Anger withholds you from love and forgiveness. It incapacitates your ability to think clearly and deprives you of the strength to make the right choices. Since anger robs you of your ability to make good decisions, it often compels you to direct your anger towards people rather than your problems.

---

[2] John 3:16 (KJV).

Aristotle believed, "Anyone can become angry—that is easy, but to be angry with the right person, and to the right degree, and at the right time, and for the right purpose, and in the right way—that is not within everyone's power and is not easy." And this is true: a wise person can be angry, anger can only turn the wisdom into foolishness, especially when they follow its impulse for action.

Road rage, a form of anger, was my project topic for a driver's course which I took in Guelph. I adapted the following incident, entitled "Man Jailed for Chainsaw Road Rage," which was written by Galen Eagle, QMI Agency, and posted on January 15, 2012, on the Toronto Sun website as an outstanding example.

It was the story of an incident between two drivers Gregory Tedford and John Bettes who were driving Chevrolet pickup trucks. They were driving east on Hwy. 7 at about 4:00 p.m. on March 25. Like what many motorists have witnessed many times during their driving on the road, Bettes passed Tedford's truck and pulled ahead of him. When Bettes passed Tedford's truck and pulled ahead of him, Tedford perceived the maneuver as cutting him off. Tedford's adrenalin started running high and he felt challenged. His emotions started running high and wild, although there was no evidence to suggest that Bettes was ignorant of his action. According to The Sun's post, the feeling of injustice within Tedford sparked a series of events that lasted ten to fifteen minutes and put Bettes' life in jeopardy.

Mr. Tedford believed that he had been wronged by the maneuver of Bettes. He decided to take steps to correct Bettes' action and express his grievance. In reaction to the perceived slight, Tedford retaliated and passed Bettes, moved in front of him, and stopped dead in the middle of the eastbound lane on the busy stretch of the Trans-Canada

Highway. Bettes had to swerve out of the way and pull onto the shoulder to avoid a collision, according to the Toronto Sun.

While Bettes was parked on the shoulder, Tedford pulled his truck over and got out. He approached Bettes' truck, screaming obscenities. In aggression, he damaged the driver's side mirror. In the process, Tedford re-entered his truck, drove ahead, stopped, and reversed at a high speed into Bettes' truck, attempting to push him back onto the highway. Bettes, upon seeing the danger coming toward him, had to reverse his own engine and accelerate to avoid being pushed into traffic.

After having gained some level of satisfaction from the retaliation, Tedford drove away, but Bettes followed him while talking to police on his cellphone. Again, Tedford observed that he is been followed and he stopped his vehicle. Bettes also stopped his vehicle at a short distance. That was when things went out of control. Tedford, filled with intense rage, picked up the chainsaw from his truck bed and approached Bettes. He screamed at Bettes and said, "You messed with the wrong Ennismore hillbilly." He tapped the chainsaw against the pickup truck's window. Bettes became terrified as he watched Tedford in horror. Tedford jerked the chainsaw's pull cord few times trying to start it.

As Bettes pulled away in fear for his life, Tedford chased him on foot and slashed the tires of Bettes' truck with a buck knife while yelling threats. Bettes was able to reach safety after Tedford fell to the ground while trying to get up onto Bettes' truck. Tedford left the scene in his pickup and parked at a gas station in Norwood, Ontario where a Peterborough County Ontario Provincial Police officer found and arrested him at gunpoint.

"The degree of persistence and the lengths to which Mr. Tedford carried out his unreasonable anger... this is awful, horrifying," Crown attorney Jim Hughes said Friday. After going through the chronological sequence of Tedford's attacks, Judge Rhys Morgan sentenced Tedford to 15 months in jail minus 46 days' time-served, followed by three years' probation and a three-year driving ban. It was a case the prosecutor described as the worst road rage assault he had ever seen, according to the post update.[3]

There is a thin line between anger and rage. All anger does not result in rage, but all rages are the result of anger. Anger is the feeling experienced when someone is offended or wronged. It is normal to be angry, and we all experience this feeling when we are not happy. We become upset when we are not comfortable with an action or inaction, especially when it comes from others. It becomes an offense that hurts us regardless of how much we might pretend we don't care.

Tedford's incident is one of the many examples of what anger can lead into when not controlled. He could have let Bettes go, and perhaps Bettes would have got caught into other trouble somewhere else if he continued with his reckless driving. The pressure from anger to fix people can adversely hurt us. It does not matter where or who we are dealing with. Think about it ... how many minutes were wasted during the confrontation, and how much danger were their lives exposed to? Someone could have died in that incident. Even though nobody died, Tedford went to jail. Why? He tried to fix someone who he considered to have overstepped his boundary. He did not call the appropriate governing body that was legally empowered to enforce the law against reckless driving rather, he decided to do it himself.

---

[3] Man Jailed for Chainsaw Road Rage by Galen Eagle, Qmi Agency; Updated: Sunday, January 15, 2012 10:21 PM EST.<http://www.torontosun.com/2012/01/15/ man-jailed-for-chainsaw-road-rage>.

Another thing is that he failed to consider was that teaching a lesson to one reckless driver does not result fixes for all reckless drivers. There are still some people who drive recklessly. Anger untamed led to rage, rage led to reckless action, and Tedford's action led him into jail.

We can sense disapproval, sadness, hatred, and malicious statements—at work, school, or at home. Anger happens when unpleasant events occur, and we must watch carefully to block the influence that goes with it. We must stop our anger before it turns into rage. Rage is anger in action or motion. It is the behaviour that is influenced by unresolved anger. Fortunately, not many angry people take drastic measures to express their frustration or hurt; however, it is almost a 100% guarantee that when anger turns to rage, something destructive will follow it.

People who can manage their anger know how to communicate and think through the consequences of any wrong actions that might be prompted by their anger. Anger, when properly harnessed, can shape character and initiate good action that can improve one's life, relationships, and career. Knowing the why of our anger can assist us to understand the what of our anger. When we find the reason for anger, we begin to find the how to better express it. This is how we can lose the venom and gain a positive outcome. When anger is initiated, it focuses on the point, but as soon as it transforms into rage, the mind is blurred. The mind wanders from the very thing that has happened to other similar events in the past—even sometimes unrelated ones—and uses that to strengthen the force behind the rage. This makes it difficult for someone in a frenzy to cool down, rage grips their heart and compels them to prove their point.

Rage is the outcome of prolonged anger. It is the overly heightened interpretation of excuses to be angry. Rage is the action of unmanaged anger and is often expressed in physical reaction, verbal expression, or emotional withdrawal. It is an extreme expression of "undiagnosed" anger that has not been addressed. When in a rage, some people may lose control and hit or destroy things to vent their anger.

Anger is a destructive emotion that can ruin one's health and destroy normal bodily functions. Dr. S.I. McMillan in his excellent book, None of These Diseases, lists fifty-one maladies that people can bring on themselves from protracted anger, including ulcers, heart attack, high blood pressure, colitis, kidney stones, and gall bladder ailments. Illnesses that are emotionally induced 60–85 per cent of the time are ulcers of the stomach and intestine, colitis, high blood pressure, heart trouble, strokes, arteriosclerosis, kidney disease, headaches, mental disturbances, goiter, diabetes, and arthritis. In addition, anger that produces long-term resentment can create sexual dysfunction in perfectly healthy people such as frigidity in women and impotence in men.

It is possible to get rid of anger, but you must be prepared to do two things: eliminate fear of people's opinions about your positive actions and the fear of being hurt again. When you are prepared to do this, the next step is to understand what anger is, and what it does to you and the people around you. If you consciously make every effort to get rid of anger without understanding it, you may never completely be healed from the hurt. Instead, any fragments of it that are left within you will come alive and grow stronger. By understanding that the consequences of anger in your life, in your body and spirit, and to other people are far greater than the causes of it, you will be obliged to seek better alternatives.

## Hatred

Are you personally aware that part of the major problems in our world today is hatred? Are you aware that the decline of peace in our world today is not because of flood, drought, famines, and disease epidemics, but the gradual displacement of love and care by hatred?

Why are things going wrong? Why are the rampaging terrorist organizations in different nations of the world such a growing threat to world peace and economic advancement, even though they have claimed thousands of men, women, and children? Why is discrimination in schools, workplaces, and society a growing concern? Why is harassment and bullying becoming a horrible menace in our education system?

The simple answer is that the four-letter word (H-A-T-E) is gradually replacing another four-letter word (L-O-V-E). Hatred is killing more people every day than any disease. Hate is, at the centre of most problems in the workplace and at home. It is not skin colour, gender, or language that is dividing our world but it is hatred.

Hatred is the feeling of intense animosity or hostility. It is an intense dislike or enmity towards another person with or without reason. It is an expression of inward, deep-seated ill will toward those who have offended us and those who have caused us displeasure, annoyance, or resentment.

There is a grey side to hatred that we barely recognize or admit that we have. It is discrimination or prejudice based on race, religion, or gender. It is the root cause of division in our world today and the very element that causes mistreatment in different divisions of our society. It is alarming that people kill innocent people because they consider them unattractive or inferior.

Hatred is an inherent emotion of human nature, but it can increase in intensity through learned behaviour. Children can learn to hate from parents, friends, or society. When adverse ideology exists in a particular religion or society, it is highly possible that it will be passed on from generation to generation. However, this doesn't have to be the case.

I remember the day in elementary school when our English teacher walked into our classroom, and announced that the topic of the day was words and opposites. The subject on comparison deals with sizes, quantity, and quality. For example: when comparing three things in terms of size, we say, big, bigger or biggest. Many of us sang our versions of songs using comparative terms during school playtime, and during the break. One of the popular songs was "Good, better, best. I shall never rest until my good is better and my better is best." Unlike the teaching on comparison, words and opposites got everyone thinking. We overworked our brain to grasp the concept and relate certain things to their opposites. Words and opposites made us realize that there are two sides to everything, one side is good and the other side is bad.

Love and hate were the best take-away for us as kids. At that age, our common word was "like." We found it much easier to say "I like this," or "I don't like this." We love ice-cream, biscuits, and candy. We like to play in the muddle puddle. We like to play soccer. We love to chase butterflies and grasshoppers. We wished we had all the time to play and less time for homework and assignments.

Now, as an adult, I can see that the foundational teaching is proof for classifying every action. It can be either good or bad, and there is nothing in-between. The situation of our world today is unimaginable. The rate at which atrocities and homicides occur is beyond comprehension. The situation today has gone out of hand and has left everyone wondering where we are heading to. Hatred is on top of the list of the factors that wreck our world today. We are battling with it almost everywhere, people of different opinion are found everywhere—home, work, school, politics, government, or community.

Hatred is the opposite of love and runs parallel to love without ever crossing each other. Hatred is an emotion which is opposite of love. Hatred appears to be the deadliest emotion which can carry extreme intense fury, just like love which carries extreme affection. These are the only two emotions, that are capable of influencing a person who holds extremities or advocates extreme action.

Like a fire, hatred can begin in the form of fear or anger. The fear of rejection, criticism, abandonment, embarrassment, and so on can grow into hatred toward the person whom we perceive to be responsible for the fear. Anger toward someone who has done something to threaten our pride can produce hatred. As revealed in the case of Tedford and Bettes, when we seek immediate vindication we embrace hatred.

Max Ferdinand Scheler (22 August 1874–19 May 1928) was a German philosopher known for his work in phenomenology, ethics, and philosophical anthropology. Scheler developed further the philosophical method of phenomenology, and Edmund Husserl, was called by José Ortega y Gasset "the first man of the philosophical paradise." According to Stanford Encyclopedia of Philosophy, phenomenology is the study of structures of consciousness as experienced from the first-person point of view. The central structure of an experience is in its intentionality, its being directed toward something, as it is an experience of or about some object. An experience is directed toward an object by virtue of its content or meaning, which represents the object together with appropriate enabling conditions.

Scheler suggested that hatred is the closing off of oneself or closing one's eyes to the world of values. He called love and hate "spiritual feelings." Love and hate, despite being opposite of each other, can be interchangeable. As suggested by Scheler, both love and hatred can serve as a unifying bond between people. This is because they share equal intensity in their individual operations.[4]

Hatred can be transhistorical, unhistorical, or ahistorical. Transhistorical is an entity or concept that has trans historicity. Trans historicity is the quality of holding throughout human history, not merely within the frame of reference of a particular form of the society nor at a particular stage of historical development. Transhistorical hatred is the intense dislike or extreme aversion, someone has toward other people of a group as a result of historical ideology passed from generation to generation. Transhistorical hatred is the most widespread form of hatred that exists across our globe. There is no place in the world that can deny of its existence in their system. Examples of transhistorical hatred include xenophobia (hatred for foreigners), the Nazi holocaust and genocide, ethnic cleansing, and every form of mass killing. Even well-respected people in a society, such as parents or guardians, can be the perpetuators of historic hatred. In many developed countries of the world, another form that transhistorical hatred exists in religion and politics. The inability of parties to work in a bipartisan way to serve the people is becoming increasing alarming.

In historical hatred, in my opinion, is any form of hatred that takes little or no account of history in its action. In other words, this is an eventual hatred, an intense animosity arising from events, clash of interests, opinions, or behavioural problems. Common examples are

---

[4] *Formalism in Ethics and Non-formal Ethics of Values: A New Attempt Toward the Foundation of an Ethical Personalism* By Max Scheler published by Northwestern University Press, 1973 Pg. 261.

misunderstandings at the workplace, club, or meeting that lead two or more people to develop irreconcilable feelings. Ultimately, they wish to harm one another because of their hatred. Unhistorical hatred is more of a personal experience and can be fixed quicker than transhistorical hatred, which affects tons of people. This is because when the people involved realize their mistakes and take responsibility for their action, they can reconcile and move on. The last form of hatred is ahistorical. Ahistorical hatred is any hatred that results from personal perceptions without any event and consideration of history attached to it. It is referred to as natural hatred, but there is nothing like natural hatred.

Hate actions as well as hate speech are usually rooted either in fear or anger, and there can't be any anger or fear without a reason. An example of ahistorical hatred is self-hatred. When you are angry against yourself based on a poor perception of your capacity to perform, it is self-hatred. Another example of ahistorical hatred is, where people who are ignorant of history go all the way to act in hostility toward other members of the society. They either attack other society members personality or cultural heritage, or sometimes mocking the treaty the government has signed with them on one's personal terms.

Teaching children to hate things is a horrible mistake on the part of any parent, teacher, or other adult in a child's life. Hatred can grow and or change its nature under emotional metamorphosis. It can harden a person's personality and ultimately spur them to do something dangerous.

Lao Tzu was an ancient Chinese philosopher and writer. He was known as the reputed author of the Tao Te Ching, the founder of philosophical Taoism, and a deity in religious Taoism and traditional Chinese religions. He was usually dated to around the 6th century

BCE and reckoned a contemporary of Confucius, but some historians contend that he actually lived during the Warring States period of the 5th and 4th century BCE.[5]

According to thefreedictionary.com/hatred, Lao Tzu proposed that, "Hatred is a form of subjective involvement by which one is bound to the hated object." This is to say that the spirit of hatred takes into captivity of both the hater and the hated. The hater is kept in a state of constant animosity and hostility and will suffer unexplainable kinds of afflictions, both spiritually and physically. This is because hatred powers the law of sowing and reaping (often referred to as the law of retribution or nemesis). The moral advice outlined in the scriptures suggests that you should settle with someone who has something against you before you proceed in your spiritual worship and prayers.

Hatred produces in us a complex mental state. It is an emotion that invokes the spirit of misfortune to visit our offenders, even as it holds us in its bondage. Hatred is powerful enough to block channels for your spiritual blessing. It does this by invoking the spirit of retribution upon the hated evenly as the hater, and in return, it is locked out from every source of blessing as well. Harry Emerson Fosdick (May 24, 1878–October 5, 1969) was an American pastor. Fosdick became a central figure in the "Fundamentalist–Modernist Controversy" within American Protestantism in the 1920s and 1930s and was one of the most prominent liberal ministers of the early twentieth century.

Harry Emerson Fosdick said, "Hating other people is like burning down your own house to get rid of a rat." Both hater and hated are subject to the torment and torture of the spirit of retribution. As the hated is being punished for what they did, the hater on the other end

---

[5] https://en.wikipedia.org/wiki/Laozi

also receives the lessons for the wrong doing to others purposely or unknowingly.

No matter how difficult our life journey is, every one of us can make a choice to prevent our hearts from becoming tainted by our world. The condition of your heart is not determined by the degree of suffering or persecution you undergo, but it is determined by the way you respond to it.

To conquer the influences of this emotion, you must unlearn prejudice, take responsibility, and develop the spirit of forgiveness. Rather than finding reasons to hate people, choose to forgive with or without reason. Forgiveness always sets you free and disconnects from the spirit of ill will. It can set the offender free from being punished by your hatred, but it can never set the offender free from being punished for what they did. When you forgive those who despise you, the supernatural takes up the duty to avenge on your behalf. This should not be the basis for forgiving those who mistreated you, instead, make forgiveness part of your lifestyle.

We all should strive to live life free of hatred. You may have countless reasons to hate someone due to the reason that we all are raised differently, think differently, and are of different temperament. On the other hand, hatred might be directed towards you. It is natural for some people to hate others but the most important thing is we should not hate them back. Haters win when they influence you to hate them back.

You win when your personality and love towards other people stays intact in the presence of hatred. The right thing to do is to show love and kindness to those who dislike you. This is an act that you must embrace to protect your mind and spirit against the maliciousness of hatred. Always show kindness, and love consciously and willingly to all, and you will be amazed to know how many blessings it will bring to you. Richard Nixon said, "Always remember: Others may hate you, but those who hate you don't win unless you hate them, and then you destroy yourself."

Hatred is a deep and extreme emotional dislike. It can be directed against individuals, groups, entities, objects, behaviours, and or ideas. It is often associated with other distressing emotions such as anger, disgust, and a habitual inclination towards hostility. Prejudice against a social group that brings about hatred towards that group is a crime. A hate crime occurs when a hater targets a victim because of their sex, ethnicity, disability, language, nationality, physical appearance, religion, political affiliation, and so on.

Hate is evil, and it destroys everything for hater and hated. Whatsoever the reason, it does never pay to hate. Decisions made out of hate usually result in painful outcomes. It does not help to hate, so let everyone accept others with love and understanding that we all are human, and we are different in certain ways.

## Jealousy

Jealousy is the feeling that breeds envious resentment of another person's achievements, possessions, or perceived advantages. It is also the feeling of grudging admiration and the desire to possess more than the other person. Jealousy is also being apprehensive of losing affection or position.

It originates from our basic instinct to continue to live, achieve our goal, and protect our belongings from loss or damage. As a result, jealousy can be a combination of anger, fear, hatred, grief, and betrayal. It embraces other core major negative feeling and can use any combination of them to express itself.

Jealousy can be best divided into four main categories: regressive, aggressive, digressive, or progressive. Each category determines the individual experiences and actions in response to the feeling of jealousy. Since every one of us experiences jealousy regardless of our position in the society, it is imperative to pay attention to this feeling in order to harness it for our good. Does it surprise you that even God said, "I am a jealous God" There is no saint who can escape the feeling of jealousy. Everyone is guilty, but not everyone is influenced by the wrong action due to the feeling of jealousy. Let's dive into details of the four categories of jealousy.

Regressive Jealousy: This type of jealousy exists when someone who has been brought up in a loving family starts to lose the norms and values they possess in a gradual process to jealousy. The diminishing of the intensity of their love to adverse situation or conditions that they are facing with, could return them to basic human instinct to survive. Regressive jealousy exists mostly in a relationship where one of the partners feels not being treated equally or as deserved, and it results in an intense feeling to diminish, withdraw, or abandon their affection or commitment to their relationship.

Aggressive Jealousy: This type of jealousy is more expressive and more revealing, regardless of its method of manifestation. It is the type of intense feeling that exists between people who are in relationship, discover that they are being betrayed and sabotaged by their partner, and they become bound to take drastic action. The actions can include, but are not limited to, cheating, attacking their partner, attacking the thing or person influencing their partner, or breaking up from the relationship. It is important to note that not every divorce is a result of jealousy. It is essentially true in the case, where a partner is betraying their marital commitment through infidelity. You will find at least one case in a week if not in a day by looking at local or international news, how aggressive jealousy has ruined lives and even led to homicide.

Digressive Jealousy: This type of jealousy exists when someone with the feeling of jealousy transfers their expression or action from their subject matter to someone else who is totally irresponsible for their feeling. It is like blaming Peter for what Paul did. Although this type of jealousy is narrow and uncommon, it does exist at home or workplace, and in the community. For example, I started my new job at a paint making company soon after the company had revised the pay scale for the new employees. The revised pay scale did not affect much the employees who had been in the company over a decade. Regardless of the fact that I did not contribute in any way to the new pay rate policy, my experience at the workplace was evident of how unhappy few senior employees were with me. "How can I get paid that much?" I overheard an employee, who had a feeling of jealousy, saying to another employee about me. Digressive jealousy is one of the primary reasons, new hires suffer and sometime quit their job. They can be sabotaged and be placed in awkward conditions because of digressive jealousy. Punishing Peter for what Paul did, or Mary for what Martha did, can also be found in second relationships or marriages. Another close description of digressive jealously is envy.

Progressive Jealousy: this type of jealousy encourages people in relationships to be continuously aware of their love and care towards one another. It helps people in unstable relationships to look inward, consider what is happening, and gradually develop themselves as a way to resolve their feelings and proceed to confront all elements of their jealousy. Progressive jealousy eliminates suspicions and judgement. It helps people with jealousy to consider what role they are or are not playing in the situation. When people confront their partner with progressive jealousy, it opens the door for more openness and communication. It improves their relationship and helps each partner learn what constitute a limit for the other partner.

Progressive jealously is probably the type of jealousy God was referring to when He said, "I am a jealous God." It is a protective jealousy that focuses on keeping and maintaining healthy union and, when problems arise, solutions are worked out by considering the roles played by both individuals. It is giving and forgiving in maintaining the relationship.

There are three major stages of jealousy, and as a natural instinct it can take any of the forms explained above. There are situations in which a new experience can add to an existing collection of jealousy, and make a person with jealousy act out aggressively or digressively. Also, negative talk like gossip, can make a partner in a relationship to grow deeply into negative jealousy against their partner or another subject. Suspicion can be fueled by concession to negative talk and can increase the height of one's jealousy. Secession can become the eventual end, or the following stages may be the case.

*Stage One: Illusion*
This is a wrong perception or interpretation of events or experiences by the senses on the grounds of fear or worry about losing one's place or position to another. Jealousy begun with illusion becomes deep seated in the heart of the person with jealousy for a long time until other positive events eliminate the illusion. This is why, it is difficult to tell who is jealous and what they are jealous about. The instinct and feeling can become so interwoven that people believe what they suspect is actually true. Fiction is reality for many in the situation of jealousy. When illusion is left unmanaged, it leads to the next stage of jealousy which is delusion.

*Stage Two: Delusion*
This is an idiosyncratic belief or impression on a person with jealousy that makes them firmly believe something, and maintain that belief, despite being contradicted by rational thinking, facts, and reality.

Delusion is considered as a symptom of mental disorder. When jealousy reaches the stage of delusion, it becomes more problematic. This is because it makes the jealous person harder to convince that their feelings, thoughts, and imagination are deceiving them. At this stage, the persons are locked in their feelings, and as a result, consider everyone is a liar and every fact is a lie. It is highly difficult to resolve the problem of delusion, which is why, it is considered to be a symptom of mental disorder. Mental disorder affects mood, thinking, and behaviour. At this stage, jealousy can become aggressive or depressive. If it becomes aggressive, it leads to dangerous actions, including homicide or mass killing, otherwise, it leads to the last stage of jealousy which is reclusion.

*Stage Three: Reclusion*
This is a form of solitary confinement in the prison of repressed emotions or distressing feelings, manifested in the form of buried jealousy that become cancerous to the inner being of its victim. The hopelessness, worthlessness, and helplessness brought about by this condition results in the person becoming isolated and eventually depressed. Self-imprisonment due to extreme insecurity, immaturity, and isolation contributes to cases of mental disorders such as paranoia and schizophrenia.

While the instinct for survival exists in jealousy, it is possible to control our actions when influenced by jealousy. It is impossible to avoid the feeling of jealousy; it is our responsibility to be honest and verbalize any suspicion we feel towards our partner. Unspoken emotion can ferment the damaging impact of our jealousy. Love, trust, and respect for our partners, colleagues, and neighbours will foster the spirit that will keep and maintain our relationship. They will help us express our jealousy in a healthy way. This is the way you can overcome jealousy—keep and maintain honesty, love, trust, and respect for others and express your jealous feelings in a healthy way whenever they arise.

Jealousy and Love
Is jealousy a sign of love? Is there any connection between jealousy and love? The answer, of course, depends on the context! This is because jealousy when it refers to the thoughts or feelings of insecurity, fear, and concern over inadequacy or lack of certain possessions results into one or more emotions such as anger, resentment, inadequacy, helplessness or disgust. However, it could assume the position of guardian of love. Whereas love is pure and selfless; jealousy within love that is inconsiderate of other people's plight does not represent the purity of love.

Henry Havelock Ellis, known as Havelock Ellis (2 February 1859–8 July 1939), was an English physician, writer, progressive intellectual, and social reformer who studied human sexuality. He was co- author of the first medical textbook in English on homosexuality in 1897, and also published works on a variety of sexual practices and inclinations, as well as transgender psychology. He is credited with introducing the notions of narcissism and autoeroticism, later adopted by psychoanalysis. Like many intellectuals of his era, he supported eugenics and he served as president of the Eugenics Society.[6] In a distinctive quote that separates love from jealousy, Havelock Ellis asserts that Jealousy is that dragon which slays love under the pretense of keeping it alive [Goodreads.com/quotes].

The presence of jealousy in love introduces vices that weaken its very nature and make it conditional. Whereas love is selfless, jealousy is selfish. François VI, Duc de La Rochefoucauld, Prince de Marcillac (15 September 1613– 17 March 1680) was a noted French author of maxims and memoirs. It is said that his world-view was clear-eyed and urbane, and that he neither condemned human conduct nor

---

[6] https://en.wikipedia.org/wiki/Havelock_Ellis

sentimentally celebrated it. Born in Paris on the Rue des Petits Champs at a time when the royal court was vacillating between aiding the nobility and threatening it, he was considered an exemplar of the accomplished seventeenth century nobleman. Until 1650, he bore the title of Prince de Marcillac.

His importance as a social media and historical figure is overshadowed by his towering tower in French literature.[7] Françoise De La Rochefoucauld believed that, "In jealousy, there is more self-love than love." Self-love is not true love, because its concern is all about how to get what you want and to have it alone. When someone is possessed with self-love, that self-love will attract other negative emotions which are self-centered and attack the existence of true love.

There's another point to make here that many people have misinterpreted: Love protects the one who is loved. It is an attribute of love to ensure the safety, provision, and happiness of the loved one. We hear people say very often that love is jealous. Love is protective, but lacks the capacity to be destructive. Attributes of love cannot be found in the character of jealousy. Love does not carry in it the animosity and desire to harm others or make them suffer in order to keep the loved one to one's self.

You might have noticed that sometimes it is much easier to sympathize with our family, friends, and colleagues in their sorrows than be jubilant with them in their successes? Jealousy does not leap in joy at someone's great accomplishment or possession—it gets discontented and resentful. The truth is that people are rarely jealous of those who are way ahead of them, and outshined them. Rather, they are jealous of those, whom they regard as being on the same

---

[7] https://en.wikipedia.org/wiki/Fran%C3%A7ois_de_La_Rochefoucauld_(writer)

level, but have achieved greater success than them. The eagerness to be in the spotlight, and getting recognized is the root of jealousy in our lives.

Jealousy is different from envy, whereas jealousy is the desire to be the sole possessor of something and envy is wanting to have something which you don't have but someone else has it. Without exception, the most miserable people in life are filled with jealousy and envy. It eats away their soul and steals their joy. They think about nothing else but having their own things or the things someone else has, which in turn leads to resentment and strife. If you believe that this does not describe you, please answer the following questions to further confirm your assertion:

i. *How difficult is it for you to allow people to use your belongings?*
ii. *How easy do you find it to compliment others?*
iii. *Do you feel good because something bad has happened to someone else?*
iv. *When you hear something complimentary about someone, do you feel the need to say, "Yes, but…" and then point out their negative traits?*
v. *Are you suspicious of those who have achieved more than you?*
vi. *Are you always comparing yourself to others?*
vii. *Are you preoccupied with what other people are doing, buying, or wearing, or with whom they are mixing and mingling?*
viii. *Do you trust the people you love, or are you always checking up on them?*
ix. *How would you welcome a new colleague whom you are asked to train to do the same job you are doing?*

When you can satisfactorily and honestly say that none of the above descriptions depict you, then you can claim to not having jealousy in you. Remember, we are required to take care of and protect our belongings, not because of jealousy but because of love. When we want other people to lose what they have, then we are jealous of them.

## Grief

Grief is a deep feeling of anxiety or pain caused by loss, disappointment, or other misfortune suffered by oneself or others. The grief we experience as individuals can either be mild or severe. The classification of grief under these two broad categories depends not only on what happened to an individual, but on the measure of its burden with respect to individual capacity. For example, if a millionaire loses hundreds of dollars, he may grieve the loss and easily let go of the pain, but when someone who has few hundreds of dollars and loses all of the money, he may grieve to the point of taking harmful action on himself.

Life is such that loss happens to everyone at some stage. Like the day and night, everyone experiences various kinds of grief during their lifetime. Loss can sometimes be horrific, and bring us into grief. Since we cannot stop negative occurrences and the grief that follows, it is of utmost importance that we learn all about grieving in order to equip ourselves with the knowledge and skill to combat the depth of impact it will have on us.

The knowledge of grief is to know the things that constitute grief. This begins with the understanding of the event and experience with clarity and precision. People with other negative feelings can mingle those feelings with grief when loss happens. This could lead to confusion and disorientation, which heightens the depth of sorrowing. While it is important to regain hope and the feeling of inclusion, solving these combined problems usually requires complete elimination of all residues of negative feelings. Any unresolved negative feelings can generate depressing emotional episodes.

Many people experience powerful emotions differently, and they retain or repress conflicting emotions, thinking the emotions will go away. When loss happens, it generates intense sadness or pain as they reflect on the past. The flashbacks resulting from the traumatic experience in the past can deepen grief and sometimes widen the emptiness within their soul (the spiritual or immaterial part of a human being).

The most common form of grief results from loss of physical life, commonly known as death. Death is the permanent termination of physical life. It is the irreversible cessation of all vital functions, especially heart, respiration, and brain activity, according to the Merriam-Webster Dictionary. Death is the greatest physical loss that a person, family, community, and nation can suffer. Death is the most brutal and inhumane enemy of humankind.

When I count all of my loss through death, I often wish there was a cure for death. However, death is a mystery that we will eventually understand in this life or afterwards. When someone dies, the family, community, and or nation gets into a deep sorrow, and a deep mental anguish, as a result of the bereavement. Grief is a devastating emotion, and the deadliest of all emotions. It carries with it sadness, anger, fear, hatred, and sometimes the urge for retaliation. Most revenge is the product of grief. Grief can make a person lose their mind and self-control. Grief can also result in sickness, and eventually death, when it lasts for a long time.

My grandmother died during the Christmas holidays, and I was seven years old then. As a family, we all had travelled from Aba in Nigeria to my village for the holiday and harvest time. My grandmother was over ninety years old, and her health started to deteriorate. She kept telling us that she doesn't want to die during the holidays. "I would like every one of you to celebrate with others and be happy, not mourn for me," she said while lying on her bed.

After few days into the new year, I went to fetch water from the Nyama River. On my way home, several people gave me special greetings. I began to wonder if something was going on, but soon I figured out that it was because I was visiting from the city. Only a few metres from my house, I noticed that many people have gathered at my grandmother's place.

When I finally got home, I saw people were talking and crying. My dad was in a pool of tears, when he broke the news: "Your Ogboo (a respectful title for one's grandparent, used for both grandmother and grandfather) is dead." I started crying uncontrollably, and my friends took me to a corner where they tried to console me.

In 2004, years later after my grandmother death, I lost my dad, and in 2011, when I lost my mom. The loss of grandparent and parents threw me into deep anguish, and it was like world has ended for me. The grief that followed left me empty, afraid, and bitter. Even as I am writing these experiences, the memories are depressing and sad.

Grief is a natural and painful emotional response to a loss of someone or something loved. Grief is multifaceted, and individual responses vary from one person to another. Grief can be connected to a variety of losses throughout our lives, such as unemployment, ill health, broken relationships, or divorce. Sometimes, it is as simple as the feeling we experience when we move away from home, graduate from college, or change jobs.

Loss happens to everyone, and loss of money, job, health, broken relationships or divorce are some of the common losses that we experience in life. While some might say their own personal experience of loss is far greater than mine, the experience and feelings of one person cannot be measured or compared to another, because we are all unique. We vary in upbringing, knowledge, temperament, and understanding. The following are different kinds of grief anyone can experience.

*Kinds of Grief*
Abbreviated Grief is the kind of deep or intense sorrow or distress that is short-lived in duration. Whereas there is no time limit or standard duration for grief, certain grief of horrific impact can be shortened by immediate contradictory experiences capable of reducing or alleviating its calculated progressive impact. Loss and gain carry two opposing feelings, but when pain of loss encounters an overwhelming gain, it is reduced to the limit of non-existence. For example, Lamar Austin said that he didn't regret when he was fired for forgoing two days of work as a part-time security guard for attending his son's birth. "I felt it right what I did at that time" he said. This story was carried by many news outlets, and many bloggers wrote about it.

According to the post by Elyse Wanshel Trends Reporter, HuffPost, on December 31, Austin's wife, Lindsay, went into labour and he decided to stay by her side during the birth of their son, Caiman. Caiman was the first child born on new year day 2017 in Concord, New Hampshire. The thirty-year-old welcomed a son and got fired on the very same day. Austin, a military veteran and father of four, had just started the job. Although he was very punctual and sincere at work, he received a text at 1:00 a.m. on January 1, stating that he was terminated due to his absences.

This situation affected his joy of fatherhood and threw him into chaos and grief, but it was shortened when he was inundated with kindness from people. People like Denis Beaudoin, a business manager from the International Brotherhood of Electrical Workers in Concord, invited Austin to apply for an apprenticeship after reading about his story in the Monitor. Sara Persechino, a former town board member and family leave advocate, was touched by Austin's story. "I don't think anyone should ever have to choose between their family and their job," she told the Concord Monitor. She began a GoFundMe page on the fundraising site for the Austin family and raised over $6,000.[8]

Anticipated grief is the second kind of grief that anyone can experience. As the name implies, anticipated grief is the kind of grief people experience as they look forward to the probable occurrence of loss. As soon as they realize that a situation is likely or certain to happen, the grief starts building up gradually within them. Anticipated grief is often present in people who have a loved one on a death bed and suffering from serious chronic illness.

Anticipated grieves are those which everyone experiences upon graduating from school, knowing that they will miss friends, the teacher that supported them, and exciting school events. It is also the grief experienced when one begins to feel about losing their job in advance, relocate from a rural setting to an urban one, change careers, and so on. When you know you are going to lose something you love, grief can kick in and prepare you for that ultimate loss.

Ambiguous grief is another kind of grief that anyone can experience. It is the type of grief in which the person who is experiencing it gets

---

[8] "Man Fired For Attending Son's Birth Is Flooded With Job Offers" by Elyse Wanshel; Updated 01/10/2017 10:54 EST <http://www.huffingtonpost.ca/entry/dad-fired-birth-son-job- offers_us_586ff2a1e4b099cdb0fd1892>

confounded, making it difficult to understand or classify. Ambiguous grief is usually set within other troubling emotions, but may not be recognizable.

The challenges ambiguous grief poses are that it could be too big to be imagined, or so small that it seems both insignificant and inconsequential. The "bigness" of ambiguous grief could come from number of different frustrating things happening concurrently. For example, when someone who just lost his job gets eviction notice and at the same time his partner walks out of his life, the grief could be tremendous. In this situation, the victim is overwhelmed and may become traumatized. On the other hand, when someone loses something valuable but it can be replaced easily, they may consider the loss insignificant and inconsequential. Another loss could arouse the pain of the previous loss and cause the individual to burst into tears. People around them may wonder why such a small loss creates such an emotional outburst.

Accumulative or delayed grief is also another kind of grief we experience during the course of our life. It is experienced when different types of grieves accumulate within oneself and form massive emotional distress capable of producing guilt, confusion and disorientation, hallucinations, emptiness, and some physical symptoms like insomnia, fatigue, loss of appetite, over- reacting, or weight loss or gain.

It's important to note that accumulative grief is not just the collection of different types of grieves, but the collection of many episodes of grief, including other distressing emotions that can identify with its pain and mental anguish. Repressing grief alongside negative emotions like fear, anger, anxiety, and jealousy is like compressed gas ready to explode. Its explosion can harm the person and spill over to people related to them.

Repressed or blocked grief is the type of grief that anyone can experience when loss, failure, or disappointment is not expressed, but suppressed in order to ignore or deny its existence. Smile on the face and pain in the heart is usually the way people choose to handle distressing feelings. Unfortunately, this is the quickest way to build up explosives within oneself without knowing it. The amount of stress we all experience on a daily basis, it's very important to process our grief and other negative emotions, as quickly as we can in order to maintain stability and a healthy mind.

The symptoms of blocked grief usually manifest faster than other types of grief, and may show up in body aches (head, stomach, or joint aches). It can transform into unexplainable sickness and fatigue. The repressed and blocked grief shows up in the form of physical ailments.

Normal grief is the most common type of grief for everyone. As the name implies, it is unexaggerated and uncomplicated grief that one feels in the course of loss, failure, or disappointment. When we miss opportunities to express love or impress someone whom we love, we experience natural grief. When we underperform in an interview or fail to answer to questions in an exam correctly, we may experience normal grief. It is the grief that steers us to change and grow. People who had changed their life from the habit of substance abuse, violence, robbery, rape etc. often experience remorse or regret in realizing the harm they caused to themselves and others. The conviction followed by acknowledgement of their doing and the decision to change the direction is what makes the change possible.

A variety of symptoms can accompany the grief and these can either show up externally or internally. External symptoms include, but are not limited to, crying, withdrawal, weight loss or gain, insomnia, fatigue, avoidance, sadness, over- reacting, shock, numbness, loneliness, and loss of appetite. Internal symptoms include yearning or longing, dreaming of the loved one, guilt, loss of interest, confusion and disorientation, disbelief, lack of concentration, preoccupied thoughts, hallucinations, fear, shame, and emptiness.

To overcome the negative impact of grief, we must first answer the questions "What?" and "Why?" What are you grieving about? Answering this will help you to clearly understand the very thing that is causing you grief. The second important question is "Why?" This question helps you measure the value of your loss, and helps you monitor the effect and direction of the grief. It is quicker to truncate the growth and spread of grief when you know the "what" and the "why."

The second effective way to harness grief is processing and expressing the grief. The processing may require deep thought about the things you have, and that give you support and help you to advance beyond your situation. In the case of the loss of a loved one, processing may take a different form. It can be verbal expression and sharing your deep feelings with friends, family, or health personnel. The more you get involved with things that distance you from the thought of your loss, the more you loosen the grip on your grief.

The most effective way to handle your grief is perseverance. Perseverance is steadfastness in doing something despite difficulty or delay in achieving success. This especially works for material loss and loss of opportunities. If you lose a deal, fail in an interview or fail in the exam, or even fail yourself, the best way to go is to try again and again. Whereas, the bereaved may not apply perseverance in their case, they can show resilience by not allowing the mourning interfere with other important people and things in their lives.

ELISHA O. OGBONNA

# Chapter Two:
## The Relativity and Reality of Emotions

How someone is affected by an emotion depends on the individual. What might cause one person to become furious could be something that another person simply shrugs off. We are people of varying emotional compositions. We have different perceptions of positive and negative emotions. We are all unique, and our differences are shaped by our upbringing and environment.

To fully understand the relative behaviour each of us has in response to our experiences in life, we need to take a look at our composition. For example, two people might have the same experience, one person may choose to react negatively, while another may choose to respond positively. The answer to the differences in their responses can be found in their character.

*Character versus Temperament*
Character, according to the American Heritage Dictionary, is the combination of qualities or features that distinguish one person from another. It is a refined structure, function, or attribute manifested in our way of thinking, and our actions. Character differs from temperament, any character that has passed through social, cultural, and moral development becomes more advanced, whereas temperament is primitive and unrefined. Character possesses

advanced features which are capable of influencing anyone's actions, and steering them in the right direction regardless of the pressure they face. Character is also referred to as attitude. Attitude is expressed in our way of thinking, behaving, reacting, and responding.

Temperament, the basis of character, is the combination of mental, emotional, and physical features that help to describe someone's traits. Temperament is a natural and hereditary unit. Our temperaments or traits are hereditary and passed on in our genes. The temperament is your original makeup, whereas your character defines who you are.

Our temperament affects our behaviour or our conduct. Genetic studies show that six individuals supply their genes to make up the temperament of every baby at conception—four grandparents (i.e. your dad's parents and your mom's parents) and the two immediate parents. Some experts have suggested that the greater part of the genes any individual inherits comes from his or her grandparents.

*The Temperamental Part of Character Formation*
There are four basic temperaments: the sanguine are pleasure seeking and a sociable type of people; the choleric are ambitious and leader like; the melancholic are analytical and thoughtful; and the phlegmatic are relaxed and quiet people. This division of temperaments is old-fashioned, but provides a basic overview that is worth exploring. Many authors have written books that give the full detailed information on temperament. I would recommend Why You Act the Way You Do by Tim LaHaye and Personality Plus by Florence Littauer.

*Sanguine Features*
People who have sanguine temperament are sociable, lively, attention-seeking, pleasure-loving, and expressive people. Sanguine

temperaments enjoy being around people. They are mostly found in places where they can meet people and make friends. The sanguine find it easy to interact with both familiar and unfamiliar faces because they enjoy having conversations.

Although, sanguine temperaments are quite interesting, they struggle with the commitment to follow a task, assignment, or job till the end. As a result, they live most of their lives procrastinating. They are always late and often forget appointments.

The expressive nature of sanguine people makes them talk too much and may unintentionally hurt other people's feelings. Some expressions that other people may consider insulting could mean nothing to a sanguine person. The unrestrained, talkative nature of the sanguine often leads them to reveal their secrets, even to their enemies, without realizing it. The sanguine are usually excited to start an activity so long as it promises pleasure or fun. They lose interest as soon as the expected pleasure or fun ceases to exist, and stop being committed to it. There is no role for shyness to play in a sanguine nature, because they are always certain about doing the right thing. When things go wrong, a sanguine person will justify it as being right from its own perspective.
The destructive emotions that sanguine people should watch for are jealousy, anger, fear (insecurity), and greed. They may also tend to be superstitious.

*Choleric Features*
Choleric temperament features include having a strong leadership nature, being brave, goal-oriented, well organized, passionate, and energetic. Those with a choleric temperament constantly try to put forward their opinions and ambition. The choleric have a bold nature, and they possess a great level of confidence.

Choleric people exhibit a superiority complex. They love to be in control of things. They are good at providing solutions to problems and are quick to envisage and recognize opportunities. The choleric do not like details because they do not like to pay attention to explanations about the nature or meaning of things. They are preoccupied with getting a task accomplished. They look forward to the end product without paying attention to possible setbacks or failures.

The choleric are hot-tempered, cruel, and self-sufficient people, and can be easily influenced by the destructive emotions of anger, hatred, jealousy, and greed.

*Melancholy Features*
Melancholy people are sensitive and thoughtful. They are very cautious and avoid anything that might hurt their feelings. They are also sensitive to other people's feelings and are very selective in their choice of words and in the manner of doing things. A melancholy person's sensitivity accounts for their reluctance to meet people or make friends; they would rather like people come to them.

A melancholy is self-reliant and precise in their expression. They like to hit the nail on the head (i.e. go straight to the point). Those with a melancholy temperament are very faithful in relationships, friendships, and business. They are dependable, selfless, and self-sacrificing. They are perfectionists and highly creative by nature. Disappointing experiences can make the melancholy reluctant to trust any stranger or people that have not yet proven themselves to them. This reluctance can make them remain in the planning stages of a project for a very long time.

Melancholy people are very vengeful. They can keep lists of offenders and offenses—including the date, time, and occasion. They withdraw from their offenders and plan to retaliate. In addition, their sensitive nature makes them susceptible to fear, hatred, jealousy, and anger.

*Phlegmatic Features*
Phlegmatic people are peaceful, relaxed, quiet, cool, slow, witty, and easy- going people. They do not get as excited as sanguine people do and are mostly unfazed about events. They do not indulge themselves in other people's business. The phlegmatic are kind, reliable, and self-content. They are peacemakers and their affable nature makes them good mediators. They have the tendency not to judge or condemn people.

Those with a phlegmatic temperament rarely get involved in things. They are shy and often prefer to observe the events happening around them. They are more of a spectator than a participant. It is worthy to note that on some occasions, the phlegmatic may try to inspire others to do the things that they would like to do themselves. They are good imitators, and have the ability to copy what other people do, as if they were the originator themselves.

Phlegmatic people do fear from uncertainty. They prefer stable and steady situations to unknown possibilities. As a result, they are susceptible to laziness, stagnation, and stubbornness. The passive-aggressive nature of the phlegmatic makes them easily prone to malice, bitterness, envy, and hatred. Predominantly, the phlegmatic people are less fearful.

The above discussion of the four major types of temperaments is fundamental, and understanding of where do you belong. An analysis performed by a sanguine will reveal that they are optimistic, expressive, sociable, and active. A choleric will know that they are irritable, domineering, and short-tempered. A phlegmatic will discover that it is natural for them to exhibit calmness and relaxed attribute; they are also peaceful. As for the melancholy, they are analytical, quiet, and wise. For further reading, I would recommend Tim LaHaye's book titled, *Why You Act the Way You Do*.

Self-knowledge is the beginning of self-fulfillment. It begins with understanding your temperament and grows to transform your thinking and maximize your strength. It is also paramount to know other people's temperaments, in order to understand your differences. Further, it helps to develop the skills that will help you relate to colleagues or manage people. All temperaments have weaknesses as well as strengths that, when exhibited in the extreme, can be intolerable to other temperaments. Self-knowledge helps you know when to give people space in their moment of distressing emotions and when share your opinions with them in their situation.

When something is not working, you can look inward and ask yourself an important question: "What am I doing or not doing?" The answer may point out the flaws in your temperament as the contributory factor. For example, if one of your temperament's flaws is procrastination, you can make efforts to develop skills that overcome procrastination. People with a temperament that slows or stops them from socializing can choose to push themselves to accept, interact, and become friendly with people. It helps you to find solutions to your personal and relational problems. Even when you can't resolve your problems, it will help you not to denigrate yourself as being mediocre or good for nothing.

In terms of politics and power, certain temperaments easily attract others and undertake political activities very well, whereas temperaments that lack the vitality of leadership may refuse appointments into political offices. Knowing your temperament can help you channelize your energy towards the right path, rather than wasting energy and time trying to become someone else.

*Distinguishing Between the Relativity and Reality of Emotions*
I was privileged to serve in the capacity of President for Christ's Ambassadors Students' Outreach at Enugu State University of Science and Technology (CASOR ESUT) for 2 years from year 2003 to year 2005. Our group accomplished great things by the grace and favour of God that dazzled our administration and the previous administrations.

Although, I did have some leadership experience prior to this position, I found this to be my toughest role as leader. I had to deal with students from eight faculties and over forty departments of studies. Another important aspect was that people were from different tribes, speaking different languages, and religious denominations. These diverse individuals were amazing people with great intellect, yet they possessed a humbleness that enabled us to achieve great feats together.
Any leadership group is liable to challenges, and ours was no exception. Sometimes the human factor can kick in and create problems as with all groups of people. This happened during our few meetings, but we were able to resolve all conflicts and graduated in grand style.

As president, one of the things I had to deal with was the hierarchy crisis between the executive leadership (EXCOS) and the general coordinators (GENCOS). GENCOS, another division of leadership, had more members than the executive members, which were occasionally involved in decision-making. It was a delicate issue, because one of the members of the executive leadership viewed GENCOS as lower ranked. This executive member, whom I will refer to as C, saw no reason why members of the GENCOS should have a right to advise or intervene in the working of the group. It played out at one of the group meetings.

The meeting had begun, and our usher or protocol members had taken their individual posts. Their role was to stand at the door and to greet members and visitors as they arrived. They assisted people with special needs and provided information to people who came by to enquire about our meeting. Protocol officers were also responsible for preventing people from coming in and going out during worship.

Every member was expected to be at the meeting before it started. C's class was prolonged by his professor, and he was late for the meeting. When he arrived, the meeting had already started, and it was worship time. The protocol officer didn't let him go inside and politely asked him to wait for few minutes until the end of the worship. C became infuriated because the protocol officer stopped him from entering the hall. He considered the officer as junior to him in rank and position. He forced his way in and pushed the protocol officer aside. The officer did not react to how C treated her, but she let the executive committee know what had happened after the service. Another meeting was called upon after consulting other executive members to address the issue.

At the meeting, we discussed a variety of things, including our progress and the challenges that were affecting our organization. The issue of the incident was also brought forward, and the majority of the leaderships were worried. They felt that pointing out that C was wrong would cause lasting issues; however, some members commented on the incident and shared their opinions. C would not admit that he was wrong, nor would he apologize for treating a fellow leadership member disrespectfully. He attacked those who condemned his action with disrespectful comments, then waited for me to see how I, as the president, would classify his action.

I began by stating my appreciation for everyone who had voiced his or her opinion, and I praised the protocol officer's decision to stay calm during the incident. I then turned and presented a theoretical scenario, considering C was in the protocol member position and another executive member had mistreated him in the same manner. After the illustration, I reminded him that we all, should respect each member's duties. I, then condemned his actions and suggested that he should apologize to the protocol officer. He stood up in anger and walked away from the meeting.

When I reached home that day, I wanted to rest because I was tired from the service and the prolonged meeting. I heard someone knocking on the door and when I opened the door, I saw someone had come to deliver a letter from C. The multiple pages letter was full of indecent words, insults, and mockery. In the letter, C called me names and said I was incompetent. After reading the entire document, I considered how best to respond and win him over.

In order to maintain the peace, I had to go see him. When I entered his house, I saw he was seated on the far end of his bed towards the wall. I politely took his permission to sit down. He was silent and probably expected the worst from me. My first words were, "I am here to apologize to you." I went on to explain that I realized from the content of his letter how much I had hurt him. I did not want to get into an argument; therefore, I did not mention the insulting nature of his letter. I explained again why I considered his actions inappropriate and what my approval of them would have meant.

He appeared dumb-founded as I spoke. When I finished explaining him, he took hold of me and knelt down with tears running down his cheeks. He grieved and was remorseful for all the mean and hurtful comments he had written to me. He apologized and asked me to forgive him. When he asked me the reason for my coming to his place, I told him that I want to show him how wrong he was about me. At that moment, he denounced all the nasty comments that he had written. He told me with deep respect that my response to him have proved me a seasoned leader. He suggested that we should dine together to seal our reconciliation. I accepted, and we enjoyed that evening together.

After that he was a completely changed person. Love and forgiveness had turned his heart around. I took steps that were contrary to what I would have done, had I allowed the emotional hurt to control me. I got a much calmer run for the remaining part of my leadership. It was lot better than the experience I would have, had he been continued the way he was. Today, he is a passionate and phenomenal leader, and I am very proud of him.

This story helps to illustrate the difference between the relativity and reality of emotions. The reality of an emotion refers to its state in the true nature, in which its attributes exist independent of any other emotion or influence. The reality that a member of our executive branch had done something wrong and refused to acknowledge it reveals what is common in every one of us. We hate to acknowledge our wrong doing. We go on the defensive even when down within us our conscience convicts us of our wrong doing. We can deny our wrong doing, but our actions cannot deny us. It stands before us and pressures us to take responsibility for our action.

People, who have been subjected to prolonged abuse or extreme manipulation by a controlling partner, may have emotions that have been warped and exist beyond the reality of the present. The relative feelings and experiences that influence their actions are often the product of the past which relates them to the present. The relativity of an emotion is the state of the emotion as it is considered in relation to outside events that may be influencing it. It explains how some emotions and their expression are affected by interconnections to past or present situations—either bad or good. When we treat innocent people poorly based on the negative experiences from our past relationship, relativity is in effect.

Due to the differences that exist between the relativity and reality of an emotion, it is wrong to draw the conclusion that every bad feeling is negative and every good feeling is positive. It is important to pay attention to the connections between feelings and past occurrences.

For example, the loss of job, a loved one, or valued property will result in unpleasant feelings. Grief, sorrow, and pain in the heart of one experiencing loss should not be regarded as negative emotions. As humans, we are supposed to feel grief and sad when we lose someone or something that is dear to us. Similarly, not all pleasant feelings should be viewed as positive emotions. For example, a man who has consummated his sexual lust through rape may feel happy about his actions. Good feelings that come from immoral acts like seduction, manipulation, deception, and cheating cannot be classified as positive emotions.

The primary differential factors to these emotions are the event and our connection to the event. When someone loses a loved one or a family member, they would be considered insane if they celebrate the event. The normal reaction would be to mourn for the loss and one's relationship to it.

The secondary differential factors are the motive and the goal. No man or woman could be justified for committing a sexual assault by claiming it was accidental. The person committing the assault must first conceive the thought of the action, decide or plan the action, and then perform the act. No crime is justifiable under the law; therefore, what one feels—good or bad—can never be used to justify one's actions. Good feelings that result from an evil deed can't be regarded as positive. Besides, such feelings are typically followed by a guilty conscience and an absence of peace.

A motive can be defined as a reason for doing something. Every motive is directed towards achieving a goal. A goal is an objective we pursue and think we will find peace and happiness in life by achieving it. For example, if you believe that you need to make a lot of money to be famous and or feel good about yourself, you will be driven to pursue money by all means both legitimate and illegitimate. It becomes your goal, but pursuing that goal without going about it in the right way leads to destruction. This is because obstacles will result in frustration, anger, resentment, and anxiety. These will keep mounting and may cause you to take drastic actions to achieve your goal.

When we get frustrated, life becomes very difficult to bear and various emotions increase in intensity. This is dependent on our individual perception and the meaning we attach to the goals. Please note that any emotion that arises because our minds have attached our own significance to an occurrence, that is different from the reality of the occurrence will turn out to be harmful to our personalities and destinies.

*Distinguishing Between Responding and Reacting*
When you feel hurt by someone, think about what happens inside of you. For instance, imagine if someone stepped on your toes and walked away without saying sorry to you, or if a colleague reports you for things you didn't do, isn't it true that you would feel hurt? The more hurt you feel, the more likely it will grow into hatred and the desire to retaliate.

Now, think about what happens inside of you when you feel deeply loved or respected—by family, a colleague, employer, and the other people you interact with. When people greet you with smiles on their faces, or when your supervisor appraises you, isn't it true that you feel happy? The happier you feel, the easier it is for you to rise above your weaknesses, give up unhealthy habits, and do your job with more enthusiasm.

In the first two examples above, the common thing that everyone would do is react. We react when conditions are not favourable or when things don't go as planned. We react when someone does something wrong to us. Reaction is common and prominent amongst all of us. In this context, reacting implies that a negative action occurs as a result of an unpleasant event. In order to better understand this concept, let's examine the medical use of the word "react." When a patient reacts to a prescribed medicine, it means his condition is getting worse because of the medicine.

On the other hand, how you respond to the way people treat you will determine how far you will go and how well you will do in your life. In the last two examples above, every one of us would respond to the good treatment.

You can choose to either react or respond to what happens. You can choose to respond by looking at the positive side of every negative event. If your flight has been cancelled, instead of cursing and swearing, you could accept that it is probably for a good reason, such as bad weather or mechanical issues. In this context, response implies a positive expression or action given in return to an unpleasant occurrence.

When you respond to a situation, you determine how you feel about it instead of letting the situation determine your feelings. When you respond to a hurt with kind feelings, you disarm the negative feelings it could have created in you. You will become in charge of the situation and will be driving away anger and resentment. Instead of reacting negatively to circumstances, why not respond in a positive manner so that your mind will be open to finding a better approach and solution to the unfortunate event?

# Chapter Three:
## Sources of Emotional Distress

The stone thrown at you can either become a stumbling block or a stepping stone. Emotional distress consists of any experience encountered or anticipated that produces extreme anxiety and fear in you. It is great to be appreciated and praised, but life does not guarantee undisturbed compliments. We take doses of compliments and criticism, acceptance and rejection, and sometimes embarrassment of different kinds. There may be no need to advise or make recommendations on what one should do during positive honour and praise, but it is imperative to know, prepare, and develop yourself to withstand the pressure, pain, and anguish that follow emotional distress.

There are three common sources of emotional distress—criticism, rejection and bullying, and harassment. Every successful person has faced these emotional distresses and conquered them to attain the height of their success. The following three categories of emotional distress will reveal and explain with clarity the three most common sources of emotional distress. They will also show you how to successfully free yourself from the confinement and stagnation of unmanaged emotional distress. They will help you recognize these sources, why you are likely the target, and how you can overcome.
Criticism

Criticism is an expression of disapproval of someone or something based on perceived faults or mistakes, and it can be distressing. Criticism may begin in early childhood and continue throughout one's life. Children are criticized by their parents, and as they grow to become adults, they in turn start criticizing their parents for their actions. Students are criticized at school for poor performance, and employees are often criticized at work. What differentiates criticism from motivation? One highlights mistakes while the other encourages improvement. The inevitability of criticism, I believe, was what prompted Aristotle to say: "To avoid criticism, say nothing, do nothing, be nothing. Even when you are nothing, something negative can be said about you."

From the following examples of criticism, you will discover that critics tend to focus on four major factors: what you say, what you do, who you become in life, and the mistakes you make. Ordinary people are less likely to be criticized than successful people. The hammer of criticism is most likely to hit individuals who have attained success or are on their way to success. The following examples illustrate further why people get criticized.

*Criticism of What You Say or Write*
On February 7, 2017, Victoria Toumit, a freelance writer, posted an article on LinkedIn which may have been deleted. She captioned it: "This Is My Last Share for LinkedIn." From this post, you will come to understand how frustration had taken a toll on her until she couldn't take it any longer. I would suggest you read this excerpt with an open mind and without judging her.

My experience writing in LinkedIn didn't do better than harm my 20 years' writing experience. I am a sensitive woman, I cannot deny. But I am brave enough to change myself if critics are just showing me a better way. I have met in here many great people. I understand what is different between egomaniacs and decent people. I remember once these two different people acted at the same time:

I shared a quote; while I was writing it, I made a typing mistake—rather than "calm", mistakenly I wrote "clam". That day I received two messages. One was in my private email with an attachment, showing the wrongly typed quote saying, "I love your quotes so much, but there is one typing mistake in this one, maybe you wanna fix it." When I went to delete the quote, there was a bullying comment right under it saying, "Can you please explain what 'clam' means?" In the sentence, you could understand very easily it should be "calm". The human brain works like a miracle.

But still bullies came under it. Some of them told me "bullshit". One found my spelling mistake while I was chatting under my article with my volunteer mother and without even telling where the mistake was (because the typing mistake was in my chat, not in the article). She called my English, "3rd grade". Some of them told me that I have a complex problem. Some said, "This article is all about 'poor me me me'." One guy came and said, "As any other liberals, when your kind of stupid people don't like some other ideas, you wanna kick them out!" And finally, one person told me I was just seeking attention and that I should delete my account and go somewhere else.

The woman who called my article bullshit also advised me to get a thicker skin. I grew up in a very highly narcissist family, with various bullies—my father, mother, and brother. Even then my skin never got thick. I always kept my goodwill. How about rather than me growing thicker skin, people tried to be a little bit kind? Why do they insist so much to seek their freedom to humiliate others? Is it that difficult to be a good person? Writing "Bullshit!" shouldn't be easier than writing "Beautiful!" or just pass by without saying anything.

What did Victoria Toumit,[9] a freelance writer, do that brought that horrible experience her way—it was the article that she posted. If she had written nothing or said nothing, would she have found herself in that situation? The answer would be no. Productive life is bound to face criticism, and there appears to be people out there waiting to take others down through criticism. That should not stop your passion to be relevant to people around you and to achieve personal success.

*Criticism of What You Do*
On December 19, 2014, Sarah LeTrent posted on CNN a blog titled "Ralph Lauren Apologizes for Native American Ads." Ralph Lauren 2014 Holiday Campaign Called 'Assimilation Era Chic', Sparks Controversy.

Chanel came under fire for featuring Native American-inspired headdresses as part of its collection that was featured during its 2013/14 Métiers d'Art runaway show, titled "Paris-Dallas."[10] In a similar scenario, Ralph Lauren had come under fire for its 2014 "assimilation aesthetic" holiday ad campaign for its Double RL & Co. line featuring vintage photos of stoic Native Americans dressed in Western attire. While it's no secret that Ralph Lauren may have been inspired by the Old West and Native Americans, and has built his lifestyle and fashion empire around selling "Americana" style, with cultural appropriation like Native iconography, its 2014 holiday ad campaign was not welcomed by everybody. Ralph Lauren's 2014 holiday ad campaign for its RRL line was aggressively criticized on social media.

---

[9] https://www.linkedin.com/pulse/my-last-share-linkedin-victoria-toumit (Accessed Feb. 7, 2017)

[10] *Chanel's Dallas show branded 'an offensive mockery' by Native Americans over 'sacred' feathered headdresses By Daily Mail Reporter PUBLISHED: 23:35 BST, 11 December 2013 | UPDATED: 14:28 BST, 12 December 2013 <http://www.dailymail. co.uk/femail/article-2522291/Chanels-Dallas- branded-offensive-mockery-Native-Americans-sacred-feathered-headdresses.html>*

Ruth Hopkins, a contributor to the site Last Real Indians, took issue with the campaign's use of Native Americans, claiming that the imagery is not only ignorant, but a harsh reminder of a time of extreme oppression, and even genocide, for the nation's indigenous people.

"What many people alive today fail to realize is Natives of the Assimilation Era wore western clothes because they were forced to do so," she wrote.

The policy of cultural assimilation of Native Americans spanned roughly from the 1800s midway into the twentieth century as a way to "Americanize" indigenous people through forced English education, sending children away to boarding schools, and banning tribal religious traditions. Some policies were enforced through threat of violence.

Hopkins urged the public to email the designer about their objections and to take the brand to task using the social media hash tag #BoycottRalphLauren.

Ralph Lauren issued a statement to CNN: Ralph Lauren has a longstanding history in celebrating the rich history, importance, and beauty of our country's Native American heritage. We recognize that some of the images depicted in the RRL Look Book may have caused offense, and we have removed them from our website.[11]

The lesson from the story is that brands should do thorough research and understanding of other cultures and why they find these kinds of actions offensive by the fashion industry. Whereas they strive to use

---

[11] "Ralph Lauren apologizes for Native American ads" By Sarah LeTrent, CNN; updated 11:37 AM EST, Fri December 19, 2014<http://www.cnn.com/2014/12/18/ living/ralph-lauren-assimiliation-ad-controversy/index.html>

popular stuff to market their design and make profits, it is their responsibility to conduct research on people's views.

*Criticism of Who You Have Become by Position or Achievement*
On December 2, 2014, I accessed a post at Yahoo news that clearly showed that position can be a foundation for criticism. What ordinary people do and get away with, people of power will be attacked and criticized for, irrespective of their age. The post titled "GOP Aide Resigns over Criticism of Obama's Daughter," serves as a good example. Elizabeth Lauten, Communications Director to Rep. Stephen Fincher of Tennessee, said 16-year-old Malia Obama and her sister Sasha Obama, 13, should have shown more "class" at a turkey-pardoning ceremony last week at the White House. Addressing her comments to the Obama girls, Lauten wrote that they should "respect the part you play," and added: "Then again your mother and father don't respect their positions very much, or the nation for that matter, so I'm guessing you're a little short in the 'good role model' department."

Lauten also urged the Obama girls to "dress like you deserve respect, not a spot at a bar."Lauten later apologized for the comments and deleted the original post, which drew harsh criticism across social media. Jessica Carter, chief of staff for Fincher, said Monday that Lauten resigned. Carter had no additional comment regarding the matter.[12]

The Obama girls got their own share of criticism because they were POTUS' (President of the United States) kids. Nobody will criticize people they find on the street, for what they are wearing. They could grumble within themselves in case of outrageous outfits, and you

---

[12] "Congressional aide resigns after slamming Obama daughters" by Bill Trott; December 2, 2014 <https://www.yahoo.com/news/congressional-aide-resigns-slammingobama- daughters-155718398.html>

don't see them on social media posts. But when you are popular, everything about you can be criticized simply because of your status.

Although criticism can be destructive, it can produce a positive effect for those who know how to use it as a tool for improvement. Why do companies have quality assurance or quality control? Why are engineers hired to do a routine check and research on product improvement? It is because customers need to be satisfied, and there are competitors who can provide better quality products that a consumer may choose over their current one.

*Criticism of a Mistake You Made*
On December 20, 2015, Steve Harvey wrongly announced the Miss Universe winner, an event known for the most awkward moment in TV history. Steve had announced Miss Colombia as the winner, and nearly two minutes later he came back on to correct himself and announced Miss Philippines to be the winner instead. Steve's announcement resulted in taking away the crown from Miss Colombia, who was momentarily in possession of the crown, in front of everyone.

Steve Harvey admitted his mistake and confessed that he had misread the card. "Okay, folks. I should apologize. The first runner-up is Miss Colombia," Steve said. "Miss Universe 2015 is Miss Philippines." The crowd became upset. Steve attempted to explain the situation to the audience and viewers and assumed responsibility for the mistake.

The damage had been done like a broken glass and everyone was left to interpret it in his or her own way. Steve, who had been entrusted with the responsibility for emceeing the event, had made a mistake. Steve Harvey's apology didn't stop at the live event. He took it further to Twitter and said he felt "terrible" for the mistake. He also misspelt Colombia and Philippines in the process. He followed up with a series of apology tweets as his mistake and misspelling became trending topics on Twitter.

The question is: Was it too late to say sorry? Has everyone attained a level of perfection that makes it impossible to make a mistake nowadays? Here is what happened afterwards,

"Was Steve Harvey's Miss Universe Mix-up a Publicity Stunt? Conspiracy Theories Begin by a Collection of Twitter Critics." This was the title of an article written by Emily Yahr and published by The Washington Post on December 21, 2015. The following are some of the claims about the event extracted from Emily Yahr's published article:

"Teleprompter was wrong. Yes, he had a card, but we all know the card is just for show… from #MissUniverse snapchat." 10:08 p.m. – December 20, 2015, said Taylor Ramsey.

"I generally don't buy into conspiracy theories, but this is the most attention the Miss Universe pageant has gotten since, well, ever." 11:30 p.m. – December 20, 2015, said Les East.

"This Miss Universe controversy was a total publicity stunt. Nobody was talking about the show until now…" 10:34 p.m. – December 20, 2015, said Kadin Zaffino.

"@kimroots I think it's a conspiracy. Mistake opens door for Trump to buy back Miss Universe if his campaign falters." 10:45 p.m. – December 20, 2015, said Dan J Kroll.[13]

---

[13] "See the Awkward Moment When Steve Harvey Announced the Wrong Miss Universe Winner on Live TV—Your heart will break for Miss Colombia" by Rebecca Rose; Dec 20, 2015
<http://www.cosmopolitan.com/entertainment/news/a51084/miss-universe-wrong-winner- announced/>

It became a viral event on the internet, and Steve Harvey became an object of ridicule among some people. In my opinion, it is only

the "All-Knowing (omniscience)" that can explain to us without assumption and partiality what took place at Miss Universe 2015 show. Otherwise, any suggestion that it was intentional has not been proven. It is ironic that a comedian who has been known to make jokes and carry out pranks happened to find himself in such a terrible situation. No one would believe him when he tried to explain to the public what had happened, because making jokes was a natural thing for him.

When I was a child, my father told me a story about a great hunter who doubled as a prankster. When I became a teenager, I heard a song based on the story. It was about a great hunter in a small village who pranked his community by shouting out for help because there was a lion nearby. The entire community came out, only to discover that there was no lion. He continued this act several times until the people got used to his trick and stopped responding to his shouts. Then, one day, a lion did show up and attacked him. He called out for help, but no one from the community came out to help him, thinking it was a prank, and the lion killed him.

I cannot say how true this story is, but this story has been passed from one generation to another to educate and provide advice. Whatever the case, the truth is that sometimes things which are corelated happens, it makes easier for us to draw conclusions.

It is important to know that as hurtful as any criticism may be, it is our duty to use only constructive criticism. Criticism arising from envy and jealousy, or that is based on assumption and coincidence, is often an act derived from hatred. An individual may choose to frustrate another without any reason, because it gives him the pleasure. It is easy to make up stuff and or to connect unrelated dots and call it a line. It is possible that a coincidence can be mistaken as an intentional act done for gain. You can build strength and achieve more success with the content or messages from your critics.

*How to Sail above Criticism*
Let's consider constructive criticism be your teacher, then the obvious question is: How do I know if it is a constructive criticism? It is very simple, "Any criticism founded on hatred is always obvious and constructive." Simply note: "If it is odious, it will be obvious."

There are no two ways about it. Criticism, that doesn't have reference points, is often baseless. Constructive criticism always refers to a standard that one should try to reach. As wise as we might seem in our own eyes, there are some things that we will miss. For instance, as a business owner, we need to be able to put ourselves in the consumers' shoes. Paying attention to criticism is foundational for creating quality products like what we have in today's market. We need to change our perception of criticism as only a bad thing and consider it as an opportunity to improve and advancement.

When you are criticized, do not quickly conclude that everyone hates you. Think carefully and analyze your critics and the criticism. If there is something true about what they are saying, then make a change and bounce back. In this way, you become better and stronger by building on the information provided to you. Successful organizations and high-tech industries grow their businesses and make better products using the feedbacks and the criticism.

The fear of criticism is the beginning of stagnation. There is one thing about criticism that causes fear in many people. It is the fear of admitting to failure or conceding defeat. Due to human selfish nature, it is one of the toughest tasks to admit one's shortcomings, but the truth is that all humans are imperfect. We all have shortcomings and will always fall short of perfection. This is the reason for continuous self-evaluation and improvement. This is why criticism is as important as praise. Criticism can be a stumbling block, and a stepping-stone as well. It simply depends on how you handle the feelings it generates within you.

What is the best way to respond to criticism of an act for which one is totally responsible? Most famous individuals, and companies that have profited from their criticism, always admit their shortcomings and apologize. How you address criticism shows how far you can go in life. When your comments are taken out of context and or interpreted incorrectly, do not shrug and walk away. People who have unintentionally offended the public with their words can diffuse the hurt by taking responsibility and apologizing. An apology softens the heart and starts the healing process for all sorts of offenses.

Companies that have offended the public with their commercials or product design have been able to retain their customers, and even gain more customers, because they have apologized and stopped the commercial or redesigned the product. An apology should be simple, but to the proud, which may be the hardest thing to do. When we get past our ego and ask for forgiveness, we grow ourselves. It can stop further criticism and make room for progress. You lose nothing from good criticism except your faults.

If you still find it difficult to handle criticism, seek advice and look for someone who can encourage you. Someone, who has had a similar experience, and who has tread the same path stands a better chance of firing up your spirit. Never repress the hurtful feelings that come from criticism, as it can damage your motivation and trap you in a cage of fear.

*Rejection*
In my grade ten science class, we were taught about John Dalton (1766–1844) who was a chemist, physicist, and meteorologist, he pioneered the development of the modern atomic theory. Dalton's name was inseparably associated with this theory. His conclusions were based on experiments and the laws of chemical combination. He developed the first useful atomic theory of matter around 1803.

Dalton received much recognition in his lifetime. In 1826, he was awarded the Royal Society Medal for his atomic theory. In 1833, the French Academy of Sciences elected him as one of its eight foreign members. In 1834, the American Academy of Arts and Sciences elected him as a foreign member. Some of the details of Dalton's original atomic theory have been proven wrong, however, it contained research ideas upon which the foundation of modern chemistry is built. He proposed ideas that could be tested by experiment.[14]

Unlike Dalton, whose theory was widely accepted yet unproven, Albert Einstein had to wait for recognition of his achievements. Einstein (1879–1955) was a German-born theoretical physicist. He developed the general Theory of Relativity, which is one of the two pillars of modern physics. In 1905, Albert Einstein's theory of special relativity resolved that the laws of physics are the same for all non-accelerating observers and that the speed of light in a vacuum was independent of the motion of all observers. He then spent ten years working to include acceleration in the theory and finally published his theory of general relativity in 1915. What a hard work!

---

[14] "John Dalton." Famous Scientists. famousscientists.org. 27 Oct. 2014. Web. 8/18/2017;<www.famousscientists.org/john-dalton/>.

Then came tons of rejection for his theory and the work. Stuart Clark, the author of the forthcoming Einstein novel, The Day Without Yesterday, notes that there was a lot riding on Einstein winning the Nobel Prize. Although Einstein had a decade's worth of Nobel nominations, criticism was mounting each year, the committee decided against his work because they thought his theory of relativity was still not proven. In 1919, when Cambridge astrophysicist, Arthur Eddington famously used a total eclipse to measure the deflection of a star's position near the sun. The size of the deflection was exactly as Einstein had predicted in his theory in 1915. The prize should have been his, but the committee snubbed him again.[15]

Einstein's contemporaries did not accepted his new theories at first. The collection of various criticisms can be found in the book Hundert Autoren Gegen Einstein (A Hundred Authors Against Einstein), published in 1931. The reasons for criticism have included alternative theories, rejection of the abstract, mathematical method used, and alleged errors due to misunderstandings of the theory. Anti-Semitic objections to Einstein's Jewish heritage also occasionally played a role, according to some writings. There are still some critics for the theory of relativity today, sometimes called "anti-relativists", but their opinions are not shared by the scientific community.[16]

On September 19, 2014, Sarah Laskow, writer, reporter, and editor based in New York posted a blog titled "It Wasn't Relativity That Won Einstein His Nobel Prize." It read: "Albert Einstein never won a Nobel Prize for the Theory of Relativity—in fact, it was only through long, political jockeying within the Nobel Prize committee that he won the prize at all. In 1922, after a long session of internal Nobel

---

[15] Sarah Laskow (2014) It wasn't Relativity that won Einstein his Nobel Prize, <https://www.theatlantic.com/technology/archive/2014/09/einstein-didnt-wina-nobel-for-relativity-he-won-it- for-this/380451/>
[16] "Why Einstein never received a Nobel prize for relativity" by Stuart Clark; 8 October 2012 07.30 BST (theguardian.com post)

hand wringing, he received notice for his explanation of the photoelectric effect. Eventually, he came up with both the Theory of Relativity and the photoelectric effect in the same year 1905.

Rejection is the act of dismissing or refusing a proposal or idea, it is the spurning of a person's affections. Criticism is the expression of disapproval for someone or something based on perceived faults or mistakes. Rejection can go beyond expression to the point of refusal. Most of the time these rejections are the end of criticism. They are absolute and final.

Active rejection is an openly acknowledged or expressed rejection. In any situation where there is a visible expression of refusal is typically characterized by energetic action or exertion of power or force. Bullying is an example of active rejection. It involves the use of superior strength or influence to intimidate someone, force them to do something, or stop their efforts to achieve a goal.

The following are examples of people who have encountered active rejection, but in the end have made it. Ellesse, a self-professed personal development enthusiast living in Singapore, put together a blog titled "66 Famous Failures of People Who Never Give Up" on his website www.goal-setting-college.com. Below are a few examples from the list:

Thomas Edison's teachers said he was "too stupid to learn anything," and he was also fired from his first two jobs for not being productive enough. He later invented the light bulb after more than 1,000 attempts.
Colonel Sanders, founder of the world-renowned Kentucky Fried Chicken chain, got his first social security check of $99 at the age of sixty-five. He had a small house, an old car, and was pretty much broke. But that didn't stop him from approaching restaurant owners

and offering his popular chicken recipe in exchange for a percentage of the pieces of chicken sold. One thousand and nine restaurants rejected him before he got his first yes.

John Grisham's first novel was rejected by sixteen agents and twelve publishing houses. Now there are over 300 million John Grisham books in print worldwide, which have been translated into forty languages. Nine of his novels were the basis for superhit movies.

Steven Spielberg was rejected by a famous film school three times. A few years later, he was conferred an honorary doctorate and sat on the Board of Trustees at the same school for his achievements.

Walt Disney was fired by a newspaper editor because he "lacked imagination and had no good ideas." He also declared bankruptcy many times. Vincent Van Gogh sold only one painting in his lifetime for just 400 francs. But that didn't stop him from completing 800 works worth millions today. Winston Churchill failed the sixth grade and only passed the entrance exams to the Royal Military Academy on his third try. He was defeated in every election until he finally became UK's

Prime Minister at age sixty-two. Abraham Lincoln's suffered a nervous breakdown after his fiancé death. He also failed in business twice and was defeated in eight elections. But that didn't stop him from becoming the sixteenth President of the United States. Wilma Rudolph was struck by polio and got paralyzed in one leg and doctors told that she would never be able to walk again. She later won three Olympic gold medals in Track & Field.[17]

Passive rejection occurs when the person chooses not to visibly show

---

[17] "66 Famous Failures Of People Who Never Give Up" By Ellesse; http://www.goalsetting-college.com/inspiration/famous-failures/9.9

or verbally say the reason for their refusal, but instead expresses the rejection through silence or sarcastic statements. Sometimes it is used by people who feel that verbal or blunt expression could harm the receiver. But when people do not know the reason for a rejection, it can lead them to overthink about the situation. Some may assume the rejection is connected to discrimination based on their race or gender.

Passive rejection can also come in the form of shunning. Shunning is persistently avoiding, ignoring, or rejecting someone or something, because of a deep-seated feeling of dislike or caution. Shunning is common in workplaces, religious circles, and anywhere people can rise to higher positions in competitive settings. It is usually, those in a superior position who shun others. They do so when they are keen to protect and preserve their position, especially when they are not ready to relinquish power.

Another form of passive rejection is marginalization—that is, relegating someone, a portion of a society, or group to unimportant or powerless positions in a system, organization, or society. For example, some companies can marginalize disabled people by refusing to hire them. When people are marginalized, they are often pushed to the edge of the group or system and not allowed to certain positions within the group, even though they are qualified for those positions. No one says anything about such a discrepancy, but everyone knows it by its recurring pattern. Social stigma is also similar to marginalization.

Social stigma is the extreme disapproval of a person or group on socially characteristic grounds that serve to distinguish them from other members of a society. While some people can cope with some forms of rejection, there is another form of rejection that can leave a deep scar and ultimately disable one's capacity to receive or show love. It is family estrangement. Family estrangement is the physical or emotional distancing between at least two family members in an arrangement that is usually considered unsatisfactory by at least one of the involved parties.

Estrangement often implies replacement of love or a sense of belonging by apathy or hostility. Lovers and couples can become estranged through a misunderstanding that causes them to alienate themselves from each another and become separated or antagonists. Family estrangement can affect people more deeply than other forms of rejection. Usually, we can fall back on our family for support, when we experience hurt and rejection. When if family fails, it becomes tougher for those who do not have other support groups to cope with the devastating experience.

Every active rejection is real, but not all passive rejections are real. Assumptions can play a role when someone is given the silent treatment. When people are kept on a waiting list and others are randomly selected, they could believe of being discriminated against or rejected. This is only an imaginary form of rejection that exists in the mind of the person who has been rejected. Imaginary rejection is an unproven or assumed rejection. It exists only in the subconscious mind of the individual who feels excluded or discharged. Imaginary rejection can also result from the fear of rejection. The fear of rejection is one of the deepest fears for any human. It stems from an act or case of believing something to be true, and adopting a certain attitude towards that thing, and believing they are not accepted.

Imaginary rejection can stop a person from pushing for something they might otherwise achieve. It can lead to loneliness, social pain, social anxiety, or psychological trauma. In the fields of social psychology and personality psychology, the term "social pain" is used to explain psychological pain caused by harm or threat to social connections. When family fail in their duties of raising their children in the right way, especially by not giving the love, care, time and the supports they need, it become possible for children to grow up experiencing imaginary rejection and estrangement towards their parents or siblings.

*The Root Cause of Rejection*
Rejection comes in many different sizes and shapes and is caused by a variety of reasons. The reasons why people are rejected fall under the following categories:
Discrimination is the unjust or prejudicial treatment of people based on "category" pertaining to race, age, religion, class, etc. rather than on individual merit. When people have the sense of being better than others, they are most likely to discriminate against them.

Failure to meet requirements, or to produce goods and services as per standards is another reason why one can feel rejection. For instance, you might feel rejected when you fail to get a job even if you fail to meet the eligibility requirements for the job. If you were a manager, would you hire a musician to do accounting job, or a banker to do a midwife's job? Likewise, if a company does not produce quality products, consumers will reject their products.

The envy of another's achievements, advantages, or abilities can result in rejection as well. The majority of leaders and high-ranking people often dread losing their position. They consistently watch out for people capable of outdoing them, especially within their circle. This may lead them to find out about everyone in the system in order to gain a critical knowledge about them and their capabilities. While there's nothing wrong with executive board members having a nice rapport with their employees, it's wrong when their motives are wrong. In some cases, people who are jealous of other people and speak bad about them, express their internal self-rejection and fear.

The last but most important reason, why someone might be rejected is a bad attitude or bad personality traits. A settled way of thinking or feeling about things that is reflected in one's behaviour can cause them to be rejected. Certain characteristics are unacceptable and shunned by people or groups. People who do not adhere to rules set themselves up for rejection.

*Remedies for Rejection*
The most devastating effect of rejection is self-condemnation and blame. This can distract you from your endeavours and paint a lasting picture of your inadequacies. As soon as rejection causes you to lose sight of your self-worth, it can utterly debilitate your motivation and drive.

When we fail to meet our expectations, we feel disappointed. Rejection is one of the common sources of disappointment. Regardless of the disappointments we experience in life, it is important that we must stay positive. It is important that we develop strong feelings that something better is coming our way. We must also have balanced expectations in order to harness the pain of rejection. When things fail, we need not follow suit, but advance. The meaning of having balanced expectations is that, we need to understand, perseverance is the key to overcoming obstacles. This knowledge will help you accept defeat, failure, and loss as an opportunity to improve.

Considering the effects of individual preference is another way to understand rejection. Human desires are unlimited, while the means for fulfilling them are limited, according to renowned economics theory. There are individual differences as well as preferences. The primary reason why committees, panels, or parties are formed is to give an opportunity to poll in order to favour the view of the majority. For example, juries are formed so that people of different backgrounds with possibly different opinions can give an unbiased verdict in a legal case based on evidence submitted to them in court. That is why judges in music auditions decide who wins based on different criteria instead of personal preference.

Acknowledging the fact that all humans are different, as are their preferences, will help to ease the pain of rejection. For example, some people like fiction, while others like non-fiction. Among those who like fiction are a set of people that like comedy, drama, action, adventure, romance, sci-fi & fantasy, or mystery and thrillers. An author would be wasting his energy and time trying to get five-star reviews for his book from every reader, or to get everyone read it.

Always be prepared for either a positive or a negative outcome. Be prepared mentally and emotionally. It doesn't hurt to analyze or have two-directional possibilities. As the popular saying advises, "Don't put all your eggs in one basket." This is because if something happens to the basket, you may lose all your eggs.

The best thing you can do is have emotional stability by reducing your emotional dependency. Emotional dependency occurs when you allow other people's opinions to affect your feelings and emotions. It is giving complete control to others over your emotions and self-image. Do not depend on people for your happiness; they can disappoint you. Your happiness is your responsibility. Take charge of your own life and do things you enjoy without seeking anyone else's approval.

Rejection is a common experience, do not become so concerned about the outcome to the point of feeling victimized and "punished." This could lead you to self-pity, animosity, or withdrawal.

Connect with those with whom you can have stable relationships and satisfying interactions. It does not hurt to seek alternatives. It gives you the opportunity to find emotional support from other groups. It is the social nature of human beings to seek acceptance and to have a sense of belonging. Actively seek and connect with people who can love and support you. This will make you feel happy and save you from loneliness.

Enhance your self-worth. Expand your knowledge, and widen the scope of your values. Add new values and improve your skills. Those who have risen in their careers are less likely to worry about rejection or dread it. They have already, through hard work, built fans, supporters, and sponsors to the point they have reached popularity. Instead of going after people, people run after them. Once you endure all and reach the top, that's it! Everyone will want to be on your team.

*Bullying and Harassment*
It's an easy way in which people express their longing and desire to belong by becoming a part of a clique. While it may serve as a good thing to members, non-members may experience hurt feelings, loneliness, and low self-esteem. Cliques are formed by people, especially young people, who share the same interests and lifestyle. People of the same religious, political, or social beliefs can also form groups because they share common interests or have other features in common. Members of cliques are closely knit and may not readily allow others to join them.

Bullying and harassment are immense challenges for the educational system and the workplace. Bullying and harassment affect the bullied, the bully, and the bystanders. Bullying can be a group or individual action, but whatever form it takes, it affects the victim's emotions and mental condition. It also affects the perceptions and attitudes of the perpetrators, victims, and onlookers. Whereas an adult may be able to handle bullying to a certain degree, students may not because of their lack of experience and weak emotional and mental capacities.

*School Bullying and Harassment*

A NoBullying.com study shows that in Canada, bullying happens to someone every seven minutes on the playground. The National Education Association has estimated that 160,000 children miss school every day due to the fear of being bullied by other students. Another research study (Bradshaw C.P., Sawyer A.L., & O'Brennan L.M., 2007) on bullying and peer victimization at school reveals that approximately 30 per cent of young people admit to bullying others, and 71 per cent say they have seen bullying in their schools. According to this study, the following percentages of middle school students have experienced these types of bullying: name-calling (44.2%); teasing (43.3%); rumours or lies (36.3%); pushing or shoving (32.4%); being hit, slapped, or kicked (29.2%); exclusion (28.5%); threats (27.4%); having belongings stolen (27.3%); sexual comments or gestures (23.7%); cyber bulling through e-mail or blogging (9.9%).[18]

One day a workplace colleague shared her daughter's experience of being bullied. Twelve-year-old Emily was different from the rest of her class members. She was smart and knowledgeable in her choice of friends, and never allowed peer pressure to influence her decisions. For these reasons, some of the class members could not manipulate her to conform to their lifestyle. There was a clique called "Plastic" in the school and it was at the "top." Members of Plastic behaved differently from the rest of the class. Their attitude suggested superiority and authority. They often intimidated, harassed, and bullied those who did not belong to their clique.

After observing Emily's unique lifestyle, a member of the class approached Emily and asked to be friends with her. Emily accepted

---

[18] Bullying Statistics; February 9, 2014< https://nobullying.com/bullyingstatistics-2014/>

her request, and they became friends. A few weeks later, her new friend decided she could not adapt to Emily's positive attitude. Emily was entirely different, and her new friend found that to be awkward. She became jealous, hateful, and turned into a bully. One day, she walked up to Emily and said, "I don't care to be your friend anymore. I wish you were dead." The words hurt Emily, and her feelings and self-worth were put on the line. However, because of her upbringing, the encounter did not result in an altercation and fight. She came home, but she was not herself as usual and her mom quickly noticed the change. Her mom started to ask her questions, and Emily openly shared her experience with her.

The use of superior strength or influence to intimidate someone and force them to do something is bullying. Bullying is unwanted, unacceptable, and an aggressive behaviour among school children that involves a real or perceived intimidation. A bully is a blustering, quarrelsome, overbearing person who habitually badgers and intimidates smaller or weaker people.

While "bully" may be the common word used to describe students' experiences of intimidation, humiliation, and harsh manipulation. "Harassment" is the word used to describe a similar action in a wider scope. Harassment occurs when someone subjects an individual or group of people to hateful or prejudicial remarks or actions, pressure, or intimidation. It may come in the form of public mockery or open disgrace.

*Workplace Bullying and Harassment*
Bullying is one of the greatest problems in the workplace today. The 2014 U.S. Workplace Bullying Survey reveals that 27 per cent of respondents have current or past direct experience with abusive conduct at work. Bosses are still the majority of bullies; 72 per cent of employers deny, discount, encourage, rationalize, or defend it, and 93

per cent of respondent's support enactment of the Healthy Workplace Bill.[19]

Harassment comes in different shapes and sizes. I have been harassed and falsely accused of things. I have had the good and the bad team leaders, and have experienced their "autocracies."

*Causes of Bullying and Harassment*

There are several pretenses that a bully might use as a reason to harass others, including: gender, race, disability or inadequacies, religion, socioeconomic status, and physical appearance. Bullies are domineering people who are filled with jealousy, envy, a sense of revenge, and hatred—for whatever reasons.

Smart people are often the targets of bullies. Brilliant students, who do their homework, do well in tests, and answer questions in class are likely to be envied by students who perform poorly in class. Some students may choose to hate them and call them by inappropriate names in order to feel good about themselves. The workplace bully usually targets the skillful workers, who do their job well, and have good attitude. Bullies are often on the watch for such workers to say something inappropriate and are swift on their feet to report them for things that they may not have done efficiently.

Good students and good workers are targets of bullying and harassment in the school and workplace. A student who is nice and caring, has a compassionate heart, and is willing to lend a hand when necessary can become a target of bullying and harassment. Inappropriate interpretation of their kindness, and unnecessary offensive remarks, can deter them from having a supportive spirit and mind. Workers with good attitudes can become the subject of sabotage. Bullies can make things difficult for such workers at the

---

[19] Bullying Statistics and Information <http://americanspcc.org/bullying/statisticsand-information/>

workplace, such as disturbing equipment settings, scattering work tools, or planting errors in their documents.

Quiet, non-confrontational, and even-tempered people can also become a target. Aggressive individuals may want to take advantage of their calmness, tolerance, and patience to treat them badly. Introverts, the melancholy, and the phlegmatic remain at the top for this type of experience. They can be physically challenged to a fight, and the aggressor will make offensive remarks to embarrass them.

Physical appearance can be another pretense for bullying. If you are tall, short, thin, fat or have any appearance differences from others, you may become a bully's object. Those with disabilities may also be subject to bullying; however, the Workplace Act, Labour Law, and Harassment in the Workplace Law in countries like Canada, United Kingdom, United States of America, Australia, and many other developed countries in the world have reduced the number of such harassment situations. Awareness of the law and social support has contributed to the reduction of these kinds of harassment situations as well. In general, any different and unique physical characteristics can attract the attention of bullies—including a style of walking, facial features, and so on.

Gender, sexual orientation, race, religion, and age can also be pretenses for bullying and harassment. Often, male students and workers may sexually harass female colleagues by making inappropriate remarks and or having unacceptable physical contact. Race has been another challenge, as certain races are stereotyped, called offensive names, and treated as unequal. Age and preferences in life can also make people a target of bullying and harassment. Some examples include: treating senior citizens without respect, smokers making fun of non-smokers, carnivores making fun of vegans, etc.

Popular students and workers are another common bullying target. Lazy students or workers detest the people in their institutions who are popular for their accomplishments—the ones who receive benefits for their good skills and good attitude. Bullies will do whatever they can to attack their popularity and reputation. This category includes bosses or those in power who perceive such people as intimidating and may become envious of their position. Such bosses can undermine these workers' efforts to rise to higher positions because they fear losing their position or being discovered as less productive.

*Effects of Bullying and Harassment*
Everyone is vulnerable to the effects of bullying and harassment—the bully, the bullied, and the bystanders. It is an experience that attacks the emotional and mental perceptions and stabilities of those involved. It impacts the behaviours as well as social lifestyles of everyone.

These experiences can affect the physical, emotional, and mental capacities of the bullied. It can plunge them into fear, anxiety and produce feelings of rejection, inadequacies, weakness, inferiority, and loneliness, as well as a loss of interest in their favourite activities. Depression can also kick in after a prolonged period of dealing with the feelings from such experiences. Some bullied, after a long duration of torment, might even consider revenge through violent measures.

Bullies do not tend to fear the consequences for their actions. If they are blocked from bullying, they may express more aggression or violence—something that grows with them into adulthood. Some may start abusing illegal substances to support their need for aggression. When they are high on these substances, there are increased possibilities of getting into fights, destroying property, engaging in sexual misconduct, becoming abusive, and engaging in risky behaviours that could endanger people's lives, including their own. In addition to these, they may become members of gangs or engage in criminal acts.

Those who witness bullying and do nothing about it are more likely to learn the way of bullies. If they perceive the situation to be entertaining, they may join and become a part of the bully's squad. If the bystander is an introvert, they may dread being a victim and live in fear and anxiety. They may choose to build their confidence and gain emotional support through substances like tobacco, alcohol, or other drugs. If they become entrapped by fear and anxiety, they could risk their health by getting depressed. If the bystanders are students, the fear of being bullied next may prevent them from attending school or speaking up about the situation.

*How to Handle Bullying and Harassment*
The video of Siahj Chase has been shared more than 18,000 times and received more than 1.8 million views since it was uploaded. Sonya and her daughter, Siahj, live in Nassau, Bahamas. Siahj "Cici" Chase was just four when she was bullied by a boy in her class. A video of her telling her mom Sonya Chase how it all happened, Titled "little girl's response to a boy calling her ugly" was posted on YouTube and then went viral.

In the video, Sonya Chase asks, "What happened in school today?"
Siahj says, "A little boy said I looked ugly."
"And what did you say?" her mom asks.
"I said, 'I didn't come here to make a fashion statement. I came here to learn— not look pretty," Cici replied. "The little boy said I looked 'bad,' and I said, 'Did you look in a mirror lately? Bye-bye, see you later, you're making me mad.'"

It is beneficial to have the knowledge of what could possibly make you a bully's target. Bullying and harassment happen to certain people for certain reasons. Your accomplishments and performance are the things that mainly attract bullies; therefore, try avoiding people who are not happy with your academic success, who make sarcastic statements about your achievements, and who show little-to-no support. This is an indirect manifestation of their envy towards you. If you sense insincerity in them, chances are they are not going to be true friends, and avoid them altogether.

Good emotional support comes from the knowledge of your self-worth coupled with the understanding of your life's present journey. Siahj knew she came to school to learn. What can you say about where you are and why you are there? A worker is at work to add value and be paid for the value it brings to a company. You are more likely to be confident and discard any offensive remarks from bullies, when you are fully aware of yourself and your surroundings.

Bullies often seek to be noticed and are desperate to draw attention. Therefore, do not give them the attention they crave, by standing around and listening to the offensive remarks. Do not exchange similar words to prove you are an equal match to them. They won't stop, if you take this stance. They will always want the altercation to intensify with back-and-forth arguments and hurtful words.

If you choose to say something, speak only a few words that cancel out the bully's derogatory and offensive remarks, and always walk away. The silent treatment may not always be the best option; however, making a few positive comments and walking away can disarm and humble some bullies. A good example is the one just presented about the four-year-old child who wouldn't give in to the bully. She said, "I didn't come here to make a fashion statement. I came here to learn—not look pretty." This clear and perfect response would leave any bully speechless. She won again when she said, "The little boy said I looked 'bad,' and I said, 'Did you look in a mirror lately? Bye-bye, see you later, you're making me mad.'" She walked away without allowing the bully to affect her self-worth.

It is very important to always report bullying and harassment. One successful case of bullying prevention is an open door to prevent others. Bullies study the weaknesses of their victims and capitalize on them to use for humiliation tactics. When a bully succeeds once, because no one stopped them, they are more likely to repeat their actions again. They may also recruit other bullies in their group to bully the same victim. If you are uncomfortable with an action or remark and you've told the person involved about it, and if they wouldn't stop, report them to the appropriate authority. Do not wait too long until you are emotionally devastated or tormented. Report it immediately, especially if it is something that has occurred before.

Always talk openly with others about bullying and harassment. It will increase awareness of bullying and the people who partake in it. Other people can benefit from your experience and become emotionally and mentally prepared to face a similar situation. When any experience of bullying is shared or discussed, other people who may have been bullied also share their experiences. Together all those involved can unanimously implement a plan of action to be carried out by the management (or school staff) team. Awareness helps ignorant and innocent people from becoming victims of similar circumstances.

# Chapter Four:
## Levels of Emotional Crisis

Everyone experiences the highs and lows of our feelings. Negative emotions can hurt anyone both ways because of capacity to influence human minds overtly or covertly. People who grew up in abusive home are susceptible to varying emotional crisis due to their negative experiences and the repressed growth of their emotions. Other who grew in an overly lovely home, may nosedive and hit the ground because they were not allowed to experience challenges that are help emotional growth and maturity.

Many examples in this book reveal what could happen at every point of emotional crisis. Some of the outcomes include depression, drug abuse, murder, genocide including suicide. However, in terms of adult-teenage relationship, many adults who appear matured physically but have premature emotions often behave as though they are adolescence.

In the following description, I have chosen to use examples relating to academic career since it is the most common occupation where adults and teens interact more often. In media, entertainment, manufacturing, politics and other high profession, interactions are more often adult to adult. This could be why in such situation what matter most are two words: consensual or non-consensual. But for adult and teenage relationship, age is often associated to knowledge and experiences.

Therefore, age is always taken into account when something goes wrong. It hurts deep to hear about adult taking advantage of adolescence, because they should know better. Teaching profession had many appalling news on teachers-students inappropriate relationship that have left many wondering what could be behind the unfathomable news.

Teachers do incredible jobs in helping children and our society becomes better through their commitment to their exhausting and overwhelming job. As someone who was a former classroom teacher, I know to greater extent and have experience how much energy, time and resources that it takes to help a student. The broadness of teachers' job responsibilities can lead them to perform the role of a counsellor, psychologist, judge, therapist, detective, police, paramedic and even parenting.

However, many people assume that a person who teaches, especially in a school are all knowing and too powerful to handle emotional influences. For decades, greater numbers of teachers have lived up to the standards and have shown discipline and moral behaviours in their career such that they were held in high standard in the society.

For centuries instructors have inspired generations, produced students that had solved life-threatening problems and socioeconomically and political issues. These for years elevated the values and trust placed on teachers. This concept and the general perceptions of educators as authority in everything may not be out touch with the reality of human emotions especially with the invention of technology that have unravel what happen when anyone become emotional and romantically excited.

In our millennium era, the increase usage of social media and accessibility of Wi-Fi at anywhere means anything can go viral. The use of computer, laptops, cellphones and internet have uncovered many hidden activities in many workplaces and has shown that we live in a world where morality has been eroded and integrity a thing of the past even to the rich and powerful.

These paradigm shifts did not exclude even teaching, journalism, medical, law, engineering and other advanced profession despite the number of misnomers surrounding these professions. This is partly because of the fact that many people tend to think that this category of elites are endowed with superhuman in brain and possibly super power to control their lives. This saintly and perfect perception can be exaggerated when measured. For example, there is no doubt that teaching professionals should uphold and keep to the integrity and trust placed them by parents, government and the community. Even teaching professional requirements demand that teachers carry out their duties in dignity and in respect to ethical rules governing their job. Academic instructors are to conduct their affair in highly appropriate and acceptable manners because of the nature of their jobs and the commitments they have towards their students. However, like what has happened in entertainment, media, manufacturing, medical, sport and so on, emotions have shown that even human experiences the same and can act based on their feeling except one is discipline enough to contain it.

There is always a moment of truth—the moment when emotion and mind go into combat for control. The moments when the very little and overlooked emotional experiences overrides the educational, training and discipline of some yielding professionals and thus result into occupational misconduct— the straw that breaks the Camel's back. A little look into the biology and ecological and behavioral adaptations of camel reveals that it is unthinkable and somewhat impossible in terms of size for a straw to break any camel's back. The expression is idiomatic and it figuratively applies to how miniscule things can destroy much bigger entity. Let me talk a little more about camel. In the contest for control, when emotion wins over the mind, reasoning is replaced with projections from feelings. This is happening more often during sale and many times in relationship. People can forgo who they are, their values and what they believe in for overriding emotional feelings.

Emotional crisis could result from arrested emotional development or emotional breakdown. The term arrested emotions may multiple meanings for different people. What may be common to some people is the term arrested emotional development. Everyone may not have heard arrested emotional development but greater numbers of people may have heard about arrested development—a term that has been used by since 1835 that connoted halting or cessation of physical development. While arrested development, in the UK Mental Health Act of 1983, depicts a mental disorder that includes severe impairment that affects human capacity to acquire and apply knowledge and skills, other researchers have argued that mental development cannot be stopped but can develop in another way. Arrested development, in psychology is no longer used to describe developmental problems but Psychiatry refers it as developmental disorder. In Psychiatry, development disorder refers to any impairment in normal developments—language, cognitive skills and motor skills, generally observed in children and teenagers before age eighteen. Development disorder is usually expected to continue and remains a substantial impairment in an individual's life. This term is commonly referred as mental retardation, cerebral palsy, epilepsy, or other neurologic conditions. The most prominent example is autism.

Although there is a close interpretation between arrested emotions and arrested development or arrested emotional development. There is a thin line that differentiates arrested emotions and arrested emotional development. Arrested Psychological/Emotional development connotes the premature stoppage in the process of growth and emotional changes that help one attain an advanced emotional status. While arrested psychological/emotional development refers to termination or cessation of emotional growth, arrested emotions slightly differ in that an advanced emotion may be flawed by overladen emotional stress, strain and pressure. Arrested emotional development may be categorized as a disorder; arrested emotion is can simply be a result of undisciplined emotions or change in mental reasoning caused by accumulated experience or voluntary action influenced by emotional fantasy.

Emotional arrest from birth through death occurs in six stages. These stages follow the word: A-R-R-E-S-T (abdication, repression, reenactment, elevation, subjugation and tussle). These stages can happen at any time in anyone's life depending on upbringing and environment. The very beginning of emotional chaos may be heightened as one goes through puberty. Puberty, the period during which adolescents reach sexual maturity and become capable of sexual reproduction is usually initiated by hormones. Hormones are the tangible equivalent of emotions just as brain is tangible equivalent of the mind. At puberty, human brain directs the hormones which direct sex glands. Teenagers experience rapid changes in their physical body as the same changes reflects in body build, cognitive and emotional abilities.

A strong emotional identity emerges not only from this consciousness of the physical changes that has taken place but also from realization of the emotional developmental experiences that feels completely different from the previous childhood years. At this point, the young adult experiences the feel and the courage to be identified by their personality, place and position in the society. This strong identity in the adolescence directs his thoughts and actions. The issues of childhood may occasionally re-emerge later from time to time and may totally fade away with age and exposure. The six emotional crises include A-abdication, R-repression, R-reenactment, E-elevation, S-subjugation, and T-trip. The following is the breakdown emotional crisis that could result into emotional arrest which may drastically bring any individual into ruin.

*Emotional abdication*: Emotional abdication is the first type emotional crisis state. It is the act of formally relinquishing or giving up of one's emotional power and position of responsibility to someone else, usually by choice or ignorance. It is similar to what happen in the repossession of mortgaged property. The common word is foreclosure—the action of taking possession of a mortgaged property when the mortgagor fails to keep up their mortgage payments. People who voluntarily hands their emotional strength to others may find it difficult to make decision on their own. They often feel like they cannot make good decision. They depend on family, friends even on a stranger the meet in the grocery store. Many adolescents grow up going through an emotional arrest. This is especially the case when they accept the conflicting roles and values handed down by his or her parents; which you are fully aware are not compatible with their adult life. Some adolescents remain in a permanent state of crisis. I must say that it is not wrong to double-check with someone else when making a purchasing decision but to completely and always rely on people for your personal decision may indicate that you are at the number state of emotional arrest. If you lack the courage to confront problems in your life, when you know exactly what to do but you rather have someone else advocate for you, you are probably under emotional arrest. In your young adult years if you had felt you're always wrong and can only act by other people's feeling and opinion of you, you may had been emotional imprisoned. Similarly, if you had failed confront issues associated with feelings in your later life and still feel that is must depend on the trend suggested by friends or partners, even when you can perceived that they are not the right things for you; you may be under emotional arrest. Adults coping with the abuse, death of someone close to them, or even their own terminal diseases, may face the emotional crisis associated with emotional arrest later in their adulthood.

*Emotional repression*: Emotional repression is the second type emotional crisis state in anyone's life. It is act of subduing someone's feelings by force. Emotional crisis resulting from emotional repression can be dangerous. It is dangerous because it can grow, build up and may explode or implode shattering the health and wellness of the individual with repressed emotions. While emotions can be repressed at any time in both adolescents and adult years; when people with repressed emotions are faced with a challenge, they may not have clear understanding of how to deal with it. This is because their perception may be clouded by their past experience making them doubtful of their capability to act on their problems. There are two major ways that people navigate their adolescent emotional crisis, they either express or repress it.

People with arrested emotion often reject their feelings because of their low mindset in their identity and self-awareness. Total dependence on people opinion may lead an uncertain sense of self and emotional repression may lead to low self- esteem. People who are low on emotional expression and high on repression are susceptible to sense of self rejection, pity, denial, and so on. They rarely go through a serious process of questioning their decision for procrastinating and will to take action. Since they had foreclosed their feelings and closed off to any serious suggestion for change; they can remain stagnant or build an explosive episode of experiences from their hurtful events. They may live through their lives not pursuing what they really want out of life.

*Emotional reenactment*: People with arrested emotions may experience emotional reenactment. Emotional reenactment is act of performing a new version of an old emotional life, usually in a way that the performance does not reflect one's current emotional status. The story of 24 years old teacher, Mary Beth Haglin, who claims to have been seduced by her 17 years old student among other stories of teachers sleeping with students can make one wonder why someone held at a high standard despite their education, training and discipline would not have absolute control of their emotions. Haglin claims that her student caught her during her "weakest moments, and she used that to his advantage." What was the weakest moment that Mary Beth Haglin was talking about? It is simply the moment of emotional reenactment. According to Haglin she was powerless to refuse her student, as she was vulnerable when he wooed her with notes and texts. Although, their relationship lasted about six months, and she claimed that they were getting it on daily, and that while she did eventually try to end their inappropriate affair, her student threatened to expose her, leaving her no choice but to stay.

If you're the type of person that loves historic movies, you might enjoy watching a reenactment of a major battle and events of the past as though they were recorded at the time it was happening. In a reenactment, people try to get the details as close to the original as possible. If you re-enact an event, you try to make it happen again in exactly the same way that it happened the first time, often as an entertainment or as a way to help people remember certain facts about an event. During emotional reenactment, the individual involved may experience heightened feelings that would override their mental capacity to withstand emotional pressure. Like in the case of Haglin and other female educators that had slept with their students, they may be going through the episodes of emotional reenactment.

This is the category of people with high on emotional exploration but low on mental commitment. It means that they have suppressed emotional maturity thereby putting a hold on their capacity to make right judgement. As a result, the flirting feelings of their teenage experiences are now operational in their current age. People with emotional reenactment may seem to be vibrant, normal, healthy adult but within they feel like they are teenagers. They subconsciously reenact their high school mood and may start behaving like their students. In academic profession, these respected educators would admire students that are brilliant, popular or those that look attractive either by beauty or out of share sympathy.

When someone has fleeting sexual thoughts about engaging a subordinate colleague in any way sexually, they choose what they like in the person and idealize it romantically above the reality as an adult would view them. At this realm of thoughts and feelings, the educator would visualize their students to be their age mates—an equivalent perception that peers have among themselves. While everyone else may be unaware of this, they may start making major decisions of getting together and plan spending their entire life together.

Bizarre! Someone may think but it is the reality of the episode of emotional reenactment. They're thinking hard about what they want to do without considering the consequences of their action. In their distorted reality, they are ready to commit to emotional relationships which precede sexual relationship. And could end up in sexual relationship, if no one discovers and stop them.

*Emotional elevation*: Emotional elevation is the fourth type of emotional crisis. Elevation follows repression in the crisis process.

Emotional elevation is the action of raising or lifting your feelings to a higher point usually beyond your reasoning such that your imaginations become the subject of your feelings. The most favorable status for people under the influence of emotional elevation is enthusiasm or anticipation. When people feel high emotional, they can dare the impossible. They adjust their temperaments and thoughts for their dreamed goal. They pursue what they have set their mind to do and press on until their identified goal is achieved. People who are on the negative side of elevated emotions, during adolescence, may experience many fears and failures that would most likely let them fit the classic image of the rebellious teenagers. They are likely going to drop out or become involved in dangerous lifestyles. Professionals, for example, teachers who experience romantic elevation towards their students may end up ruining their career and marriage for it.

A classic example is romantic relationship between Jennifer Marie Mason, 30 and her student. The boy was 14 when the relationship began and 16 when it was discovered and reported to police. It was reportedly that when Mason was on her honeymoon in Europe in the summer of 2012, she emailed the boy numerous times. After she returned, they met and kissed at a public park. A year later, according to the Crown prosecutor, Vicki Faulkner, Mason sent him a happy birthday greeting that said: "I'm yours forever, you own my heart, you rule my world, you are my king, my best friend, my lover, forever. I love you more than you will understand."

Mason key words are, my heart, my world, my king, my best friend, my lover, forever and more than you understand. Mason, a former Calgary Catholic school teacher was sentenced to two years in federal prison and must be registered as a sex offender for 20 years after she pleaded guilty to sexual exploitation for an illicit sexual affair with a teenager male student. [Source: Daryl Slade, Post Media News, National Post]

The fact that Mason expressed her feeling to her students in this manner suggests that she was completely sold out to the teen despite of the fact that she was his teacher and about a double of his age. She idealized him romantically and affectionately and was willing to sacrifice her marriage for it. This fourth level of emotional crisis is blindfolding. It takes the individual far away from reality and consequences of their action. At this stage of crisis, age identity diffuses as the individual live in the fantasy that may cause them to experience difficulties recognizing the legal implications and the damaging effect of their unacceptable behavior toward their victim.

*Emotional subjugation*: Subjugation is the fifth type of emotional crisis. Emotional subjugation is the action of bringing someone soul under the domination or control of their feelings. When human minds and willpower becomes subdued by heightened feelings, their capacities to oppose inappropriate feeling becomes weakened and paralyzed. This is especially the case with Instructors who sleep with their students. They tend to lose the consciousness that there are chances of impregnating or becoming impregnated by the students. Christine Scarlett, 40, took the chances and the end result was unimaginable. Scarlett pleaded guilty to five felony charges for her seduction of 17 years old Steven Bradigan, who happened to be captain of the Strongsville High School football team when the relationship began in 2002. She also gave birth to his son in 2003.

Emotional subjugation is turbulent emotional crisis. It is the areas for which negative feelings engage in some serious dangerous exploration. Continuing on the path will set one up for irreconcilable damage. People under the influence of emotional subjugation tend to float in the distorted reality of heightened feelings, when they become subjugated to their feelings, they may be led astray and become the subject of their world. They lose control of their mind and self into high-risk behaviors even into murder. The story of Pamela Smart is that example. She impressed a group of high school freshmen with her love of metal music; she then began an affair with one of them. She was having an affair with freshman Billy Floyd. After her husband was found shot to death, she and Billy Floyd, along with three Floyd's friends, were arrested on suspicion of the shooting. During trial, the prosecution claimed that Smart had coldly plotted to seduce Floyd and convinced him to murder her husband. Smart maintained that Floyd shot her husband of his own accord, after she threatened to end their affair.

*Emotional tussle*: emotional tussle take place at different interval in the process and may continue after every other state has been experienced. It is the most floating emotional crisis. Emotional tussle is the vigorous struggle or scuffle people in emotional crisis experience as their feeling contest for control and influence. Emotional tussle is perhaps the most delicate stage of emotional arrest and crisis. People in the emotional tussle status that are discovered and stopped may likely go through the cycle of emotional experiences and continue their exploration of their past and present before they're forced to give in to one direction. The problem with the tussle status is that the longer the people with this condition float on the realm of their fantasy and struggle with its overwhelming imports. They are less likely to regain their sense of self-image enough to redirect their behavior. Emotional tussle is not a one- time thing. It can happen many times in the episode of emotional crisis.

During this stage, both adolescents and adults are faced with the challenges of integrating the ideas of themselves, how they feel and about other people opinion of them. As a result, many form their self-image and endure the task of resolving their emotional tussle with the reality of their self-identity. For example, Pamela Rogers Turner was 27 and an elementary school teacher coach when she was arrested in

February 2005 for having an ongoing relationship with a 13 years old student. In August of 2005, she pleaded no contest to charges of sexual battery by an authority figure and was sentenced to 9 months in prison, as part of an 8-year suspended sentence for statutory rape. In April 2006, she was arrested for turning around and doing it again— this time for sending sexual pictures and videos of herself to the same student and trying to contact him through the internet.

Successful resolution of the emotional tussle depends on one's progressive emotional triumph over negative experiences through dynamic positive emotional development acquired through awareness, acceptance and self- control. Sometimes people face obstacles that may attack their emotional stability and prevent them from developing a strong and viable emotional capacity to maintain their personal identity. This sort of emotional tussle leaves individuals struggling to "find themselves". They are thrown into confusion and often seem to have no idea who or what they are, where they belong or where they want to go. They may withdraw from normal life, not taking action or acting as they usually would at work, in their marriage or at school, or be unable to make defining choices about the future. They may even turn to negative activities, such as crime or drugs as a way of satisfying their desire for self-approval.

On the other side of the spectrum, people who learned to resolve their emotional tussle from the adolescent stage usually step into adulthood with a strong sense of identity. They emerge well equipped to face adulthood with confidence as a result of their expertise in handling emotional crisis. It is usually easy to weather the storm and a spill into adulthood would hamper emotional development. Any strong impact on emotional development during adolescence association with negative emotional tussle that went unresolved may result into bias personality. Many individuals that had gone all the way to join groups such as cults or fanatics may have had issues developing stable and balanced emotional status during this fragile time.

# Chapter Five:
## The Five Laws of Emotions

Laws are statements of facts, deduced from observation, to the effect that a particular natural or scientific phenomenon always occurs if certain conditions prevail. The laws of emotions explain the characteristics of human emotions at different states. It explains how feelings influence us and what happens when we take action either for or against the feeling we experience. We are emotional beings and feel a variety of emotions every day of our lives, it is important to have the knowledge of these laws. We need to keep our emotions in order to avoid the possible dangers that are clinging to negative emotions. The five laws of emotions include: expression, repression, transmutation, transference, and diminishing return. Each law of emotion has factual and particular forms of procedure in accomplishing a systematic or established end. These are simple principles and universally applicable facts that do not change, regardless of geographical location or a person's ethnicity. There are always consequences for breaking these emotional laws like other laws. But breaking emotional laws can have slow, deteriorating, negative effects, unlike penalties of constitutional and other laws.

When you break written laws or bylaws you pay for it. You may have to pay a fine, provide restitution, face a suspension, or even serve jail time. The prosecutor has the duty to serve you notice, tell you what you did, and prove that you have broken the law. You can then protest, invoking your right of due process. If you are found not guilty, you will be acquitted. However, when you break emotional laws, you may shrug it off and go about your business. There is no physical enforcement officer or prosecutor to charge you or take you to the court of law, you appear to be off the hook. But are you truly off the hook? The answer is no.

Breaking emotional laws usually has an adverse effect on us. We can never escape its consequences unless we do something that will force them to grant us parole. Keeping the conditions of the parole and doing what it requires is the only way to freedom. The following are the five major laws of emotions with detailed information.

*The Law of Expression*
The Law of Expression of Emotion states: *The rate at which an emotion is expressed is directly proportional to the depth of the impression influencing it. And the expression of an emotion can reproduce another of its kind or even more unless intercepted by greater force.*

Emotion is expressed to outwardly manifest a mood or disposition because of an event or a series of experiences that one has unconsciously stored within. When an emotion is expressed, two things happen. First, the offender is informed and becomes aware of their actions. This could put an end to any further offenses, especially if the offender acknowledges what they have done. Secondly, you release the negative energy built up by the experience. If the offender does not accept responsibility, you cannot be reconciled to them; however, by expressing the hurtful feelings, you release the energy even if the thought of the experience may still be there. The hurtful feeling expression could involve the act of transferring an interpretation of what is felt inwardly into spoken words or action. When an emotion is expressed, it reveals one's character or feelings.

The expression of emotion includes the manner or form in which a thing is expressed. For example, when you say "I love you" the facial expression and the voice will be different from the one when you say "I hate you; get out of here." Likewise, tears falling from someone's eyes indicate that he or she is sad (or sometimes very happy or moved), and a pleasant countenance is an indication that a person is happy with an outcome. Our emotions always seek means to be expressed with or without words. When an emotion is not expressed verbally, it can still be expressed through body language to show that one is aggressive, assertive, attentive, bored, confident, defensive, submissive, etc.

When someone is angry and chooses not to express it by the means available to them, they subject themselves to apathy (absence or suppression of emotion). Anger is masked in apathy, and the wish to retaliate remains—although under the cover of passive indifference. One might resort to using assertive body language instead of aggressive body language. The person loses control of emotions and responds with violence.

Most times, you do not stop at one punch. For example, after the first time when a wife calls her husband "stupid," she is likely to use more abusive names. In the same manner, if a husband punches his wife once, he will likely continue to use violence against her.

If you are likely to use violence or profane or abusive language when provoked, it is advisable for you to immediately walk away from the scene, when you sense your emotions rising. When you are hurt, do not be too quick to express it. Instead, give yourself some time to allow yourself to think, how to best express your emotions without creating more problems for yourself or the person who has hurt you. People, who have saved their immediate response to anger for a few minutes, can testify to the fact that they saved themselves from big trouble by doing so.

This does not mean that every time you are hurt, you hold onto your emotions. Sometimes you need to speak up and express your feelings of hurt or disagreement to a wrongdoing openly. When you believe something is not right and keeping your mouth shut will cause someone to get into danger or suffer. You don't have to be judgmental, but be frank about the unpleasantness of a situation. In such a situation, your silence is an indication of your lack of love or caring. In certain situations, you need to express your feelings openly and wisely. This will help you avoid turning your hurt into anger, which could cause you to do something terrible. Whenever you speak up, always remember that you do not have control over the behaviour of other people or the choices, they make about their way of life.

It is important to note that, what influences people appeals to their emotion. Influence is the capacity of a thing, event, action, or behaviour to produce an effect on you. It is the power that sways or affects you without any direct or apparent effort. People are influenced in different ways, but for an influence to be possible, it must captivate your emotions before it can produce a result.

This is what differentiates successful salespeople from unsuccessful ones. Successful salespeople use this tool to market their product. They know that two key things drive a consumer—the price of the product and the benefits or utility that the product offers. The companies compare prices, quality, and utility with their competitors in a manner that will appeal to the emotions of their prospective client. Once the client's emotion connects to their expression, it becomes irresistible for the client to say no.

The three laws of motion developed by Isaac Newton, apply to every motion except e-motion. This is because while every feeling does to some extent produce a force, we can choose to accept or ignore the effect it produces on us because of our intellect. But if this effect or force is powerful enough to override our mind's power, it can influence our actions.

For example, a smile is a facial expression that indicates pleasure, acceptance, or friendliness. Yet you still can meet people who will choose not to smile back at you when you smile at them. If you have experienced this, you will agree with me that the smile you are offering will go away abruptly to this reaction. There are some people whose experiences in life have stolen from them the capacity to show happy feelings. People of this kind need more time to be influenced to smile back. Transformation does not often happen in an instant.

Sometimes you may experience a conflict of emotions—a state of disharmony or opposition that exists between two or more emotions and that results in discord. Since negative and positive emotions are not compatible, there is a struggle whenever the two occur at the same time. Each of the emotions strives to achieve its dominion over the other by appealing to the mind and interests of the person involved. The emotion that connects more strongly with the individual wins. For instance, if the individual involved is weak-willed and lacks the necessary knowledge to set boundaries and make the right choices, or if he does not have principles, values, or rules guiding his life, the more negative emotions are likely to come out on top. It then becomes the dominating influence in that individual's life until a stronger emotion overpowers it.

In any challenging situations, we are often faced with two questions with regards to how to express our feelings: The first is, why should I let him go free after hurting me so deeply? The second is, how am I sure he won't do the same thing again or take me to be a weakling? As these questions are going on in your mind, anger and the virtue of kindness may show up, each pointing out why you should or shouldn't teach the other person a lesson. If your mind does not quickly provide the right answer to what you should do, anger will go back into your memories to draw up past similar experiences, whereas patience will use your inward knowledge to provide insight into the consequences should you react to the situation. As the two emotions continue the struggle to save or destroy you, anger will keep urging you, "Deal with him. Who the hell does he think he is?" However, love will keep saying, "Don't hurt him back. You may choose to tell him now or later, but with the correct measure and attitude in mind."

*The Law of Repression*
Repression of an emotion can be defined as the act of controlling a strong or dominating feeling by trying to ignore it or hold it. It is also a conscious or an unconscious exclusion of a feeling of hurt or pleasure from the conscious mind. Repressed emotion causes long-term effects. It takes a long time and lots of energy to repress emotion. Repressed emotions can degrade our physical body and strength and cause serious illness and health problems.

The Law of Repression of Emotion states: *Every repressed emotion stays alive and usually finds expression inwardly or outwardly by remonstrance, and/or deterioration of the body (health).*

Repressed emotion is a living but as a suppressed emotion, since emotion cannot be buried. It functions at the unconscious level in your system, where it will start to develop the need to retaliate either directly or indirectly. As this urge grows in strength, it will either consciously or unconsciously begin to influence you. It may cause you to start doing things that you would not normally do, and you may find your own behaviour baffling. Over time, repressed emotions will impede your motivation and drive to be successful in life. Repressed emotions hinder growth and development.

For example, if a child has been abused and has repressed his feelings about this trauma until adulthood, at some point he may unconsciously start acting strangely or doing things that have never been a part of his life. The individual may not figure out the foundation and reason for the sudden change in behaviour. The person will likely realize that certain experiences of the past that have been repressed are now showing up in his life, and that wrong was done to him during his childhood. For instance, an adult who was either abused or whose parents were very demanding might find he has developed a strong feeling of hatred and anger towards his parents. This may also happen when a person is still young, and they might start failing in school because of the repressed feelings against their parents.

Every adult should look inward and, in the past, to determine why he or she behaves in a certain way. Many homes are plunged into discord and unhappiness because of repressed offenses of the past. A wife who is harbouring hurt from her parents' home may now be nagging or insulting her husband as a result. In the same vein, a husband may physically abuse his wife because of repressed feelings he is still harbouring from his childhood home.

Stains that are not washed away can spread to other areas. Emotions that are buried alive attract other feelings of a similar kind, and these can grow within you. The negative and positive emotions cannot cohabit in the same body, the hurt that already exists will always overshadow any opportunities for delight.

Repressed emotion has an elastic limit, and beyond this limit it finds expression in internal revolt that can become progressively worse. This is because within your unconscious mind, repressed emotion builds itself up by reproducing new feelings of the same kind from fragments of existing feelings of hurt or new hurts. There is a limit to which you can repress emotion. Those who specialize in ignoring or suppressing their feelings are susceptible to feelings of revenge. How long an emotion will stay repressed is hard to say, but once it has exceeded a certain limit, it becomes difficult for it to return to normal. It may either explode or change your lifestyle. When it exceeds its elastic limit, any little thing might ignite it, and anyone who does not agree with you becomes your enemy.

*The Law of Transmutation*
Transmutation of emotion can be defined as a system or phenomenon by which the form of our feelings is changed into another. Feelings can undergo a change and become different in essence. When a feeling is changed, it may lose its original nature yet still carry its strength into its new form or character.

The Law of Transmutation of Emotion states: *Feelings cannot be created or destroyed, but their energy can be redirected from their original use to another and/or be combined with other feelings to form a synergy.*

Feelings can be transmuted or changed through a conscious technique that one must purposely and willingly employ to achieve the required change. A strategic action undertaken to gain this end must follow the right procedure for a total change to happen. Since it is not advisable to repress feelings or express them negatively, it is paramount to follow a principle that will cause a successful transformation. This way, you will be able to consciously redirect the power of negative emotions into a positive form.

To further explain how this works, let us look at the various forms in which energy exists and how these can be channeled through devices that convert them to another form of energy. Forms of energy include light, electrical, heat, solar, hydro, mechanical, etc. For example, electrical energy is converted to light energy using a device called an electric bulb. You can do something similar by redirecting the power behind an emotion. With successful redirection, you can change the nature of your feelings.

Consider fear, which can stimulate the "flight or fight" response in your body. If the strength and vigour from this response can be consciously directed to a different activity, it can be used to achieve a goal that one has set for oneself. Likewise, anger, which also stimulates the mind, can be redirected towards positive activities.

Since emotion is not something that can be physically handled, the tool you must use to redirect or transmute it, is the power of knowledge. Mastering the power of your mind and developing its capacity to identify your feelings and channelize the power to more positive ones can make you successful in life. You can learn how to take your mind off negative emotions (anger, hatred, fear, etc.) and direct their strength to positive emotions (enthusiasm, love, confidence, etc.). The strength of negative emotions can also be directed towards one's career or personal life.

Transmutation happens through intense mental concentration. Successful politicians, salespeople, business people, and others often attain their success by either consciously or unconsciously transforming the power of their emotions thereby creating a strong synergy that drives their passion and career forward. Just as a young man driven by a crush might find the confidence to approach a girl to ask her out, or salespeople who have mastered the ability to redirect their emotions, approach potential customers with the confidence and enthusiasm. This does not happen by chance, but rather through knowledge and practice. They develop the skill and confidence to approach "strangers" and appeal to their emotions by explaining the benefits and quality of the product they want them to buy. In doing so, they master sales skills, which include connecting a sale to a customer's emotions.

There are three steps to achieving this skill: knowledge, acceptance, and commitment. By reading this book, you are beginning step one. You need to accept this knowledge to be true and commit yourself to practicing the skill. In doing this and through consistent application, you will start seeing the results you desire. It is important to add that in commitment, there's the need for a bold declaration, which will help boost your confidence when you are faced with rejection. This takes us to two key points about redirection and transmutation—the Principle of the Persistence of Emotion and the Principle of Displacement.

The Principle of the Persistence of Emotion explains that positive, persisting emotion wears down resisting (negative) actions—such as bad habits. The scriptures state: *"Do not be overcome by evil, but overcome evil with good"*.[20] A habit once developed can be difficult to stop, but by following the Principle of Persistence, you can erode a resisting habit. Since a habit is an unconscious pattern of behaviour that is acquired through frequent repetition, cultivating positive emotions and opposing a bad habit with good emotions can help you put a stop to it. Though it might take time, it is guaranteed to work as long as you don't give up.

Similarly, at your place of work you can resist evil actions with good ones. You can win over those who are bent on hurting you by continuously showing them love, kindness, and care. It will not be long before evil will bow at the feet of good deeds. This is because both natural laws—the Law of Sowing and Reaping and the spiritual law (the law of the Spirit of Life)—will kick in to deliver victory into

---

[20] Romans 12:21 (NIV)

your hands. The scriptures say, *"... the same measure that you mete withal it shall be measured to you again"*.[21] This law will automatically come into play, and it will amaze you how everything will turn out for the best.

Next is the Principle of Displacement. This explains the process by which one or more similar emotions take the place of another emotion(s). This may be achieved either by gradual effort or by force—as some negative emotions can become so attached to a person's core that they do not go easily. Thus, when an individual is affected by a strong and negative emotion, it becomes paramount to invite a stronger, positive emotion to deal with it. The stronger emotion will overpower, disarm, and move it away from your life. When two contesting emotions meet each other and strive for dominancy, it is the stronger or more equipped emotion that wins. It is important to note that what makes one emotion stronger than the other is dependent on the nature of the system they are striving to occupy. For example, it is easier for those who trust and believe in God to operate in faith than it is for those who deny his existence and power. When faith and fear strive for space in the life of a carnal man, fear always wins, because a carnal man's nature is more susceptible to fear than a spiritual person.

Joy and sorrow cannot cohabit. Love and hatred cannot be in fellowship. When one shows up, the weaker emotion gives way. Also, if an emotion needs constant reinforcement, such emotion can grow cold. For example, faith (which exists as an emotion at the level of hope) can be reinforced by the power of believing and speaking out about this belief. When disbelief sets in and speaking boldly ceases, fear will creep in and dominate the individual. How much faith you have and how well you reinforce it determines the degree of resistance it will put up against the enemy called fear.

---

[21] Luke 6:38 (KJV)

*The Law of Transference*
Transference of emotion is the phenomenon by which emotions or desires originally associated with one person, such as a parent or sibling, are either consciously or unconsciously shifted to a new person. It includes the transfer of an emotion(s) unconsciously retained from a past experience towards a new person or thing. Transference occurs in many ways some of which we may not be aware. For example, a friend might remind you of your hated grade six teacher, so you cringe in fear around your friend in remembrance of your hard and hurtful experiences with your teacher. This is transference of emotion.

The Law of Transference of Emotion states: *The degree of moving or shifting feelings from one object to another (e.g., from one person to another person) is directly proportional to the willingness and openness of the sender and the knowledge and capacity of the recipient.*

When someone impacts you with a philosophy, ideas, and or experiences in such a manner that you start having certain feelings, transference has taken place. This explains why people who are frustrated or stressed out often seek to vent their anger. As soon as someone or something gets the heat of it, they feel better. It is also the reason, why those who suffer from depression, are often asked to share their feelings with someone. It is important to share feelings. When feelings are shared, transference takes place. Feelings are put away and sometimes completely released in the process of transference. Some people can attest to the fact that when they share their pain with someone—even if that person doesn't have any advice or solutions to offer—they get some level of relief because they found ears that listened.

In some cases, the one who hears the pain can be so impacted by it that they may develop intense feelings about the situation and want to respond or take over the matter themselves. Whichever way it happens, transference does happen almost every day at home and work, in the community, and while watching television, listening to music, and so on.

The problem with human-to-human emotional transference is that the process is rarely completed because of distractions. Also, there may be some spiritual element involved when an individual is hurt. This is why spiritual activities such as prayer, worship, and meditation may be required to take care of a spiritual disturbance that has occurred as a result of the hurt.

*The Law of Diminishing Returns of Emotional Hurt*
In economics, diminishing returns (also called The Law of Diminishing Marginal Returns) states that in all productive processes, adding more of one factor of production while holding all others constant (ceteris paribus) will at some point yield lower per unit returns.

In physics, Hooke's Law (1676) states that the deformation of a body is proportional to the magnitude of the deforming force, provided that the body's elastic limit is not exceeded. If the elastic limit is not reached, the body will return to its original size once the force is removed.

These two laws apply to what happens to our human systems emotionally, mentally, and physically when a deforming force (hurt, trauma, abuse, etc.) is consistently applied to our lives, provided that we do not increase our capacity to deal with or redirect the negative force. At some point, it will cause deformation to a part of or our whole system if it is not removed.

The Law of Diminishing Returns of Emotional Hurts states: *When negative, bad, or hurtful feelings are increased by corresponding hurtful events, and the capacity to cope, tolerate, or deal with them are held constant, the resultant effect, after a certain time, will eventually diminish a part of or the whole of the body— mentally and/or emotionally.*

The Law of Diminishing Returns is the law that explains how hurt and intense sadness may sometimes result in depression. When we don't build our capacity to understand how emotion works, when we don't increase our knowledge-bank about hurt. And when we cannot accept that forgiveness is necessary to be free from hurt, we become susceptible to a possible breakdown from the continuing hurts in our lives.

You will no doubt agree with me that hurt is sometimes inevitable. As long as you are alive and encountering other people, there is no way you can completely escape being hurt. People hurt each other, either deliberately or inadvertently, but it is inevitable. Your hairdresser could misinterpret your instructions and not give you the hairstyle you desired. Your team leader may ignore your hard work and complain about you without any good reason. Your spouse may oppose your decisions, and the list goes on and on.

It is necessary to clean your heart of any hurt, just like it is necessary for you to wash the dirt from your clothing to keep it clean and neat. Why does our clothing get dirty? It is from contact—contact with sweat, dust, oil, grease, etc. Likewise, our feelings get hurt when we interact with people.

If you have a history of abuse and losses, or if you have been neglected by your family for no obvious reason, or if you have been rejected, you must accept the fact that this law carries with it that stored up hurt, which is disastrous both to the body and mind. It has the capacity to eat into the fabric of your system and erode your emotional, mental, and physical health and wellness.

What do you need to do? You need to build your capacity to deal with hurt through knowledge. You need to always send your heart and emotions to a laundromat. If you are aware of the dangers of keeping hurt alive, you can avoid giving room in your heart for the hurt. Strive to resist any reason that suggests you pile up hurt. Do not keep records of hurts. This only compounds the hurt, and unless checked, it will ruin you.

# Chapter Six:
## The Grip of Depression

Depression is a condition characterized by feelings of extreme gloom and inadequacy. Common symptoms include the inability to concentrate or experience pleasure; disturbances of sleep and appetite; feelings of sadness, guilt, helplessness, hopelessness; and thoughts of death. It is both an emotional and mental impairment of the normal psychological and physiological functions of someone's system, which can cause an individual to feel worthless, lonesome, and dejected and gets plunged into an intense prolonged sadness that is not justifiable by any objective reason. It can lead to withdrawal from friends and family members.

As we go through life, we all encounter events that hurt our feelings. Every one of us is in a constant battle with feelings of extreme sadness, guilt, and helplessness. When we are not able to combat such feelings for prolonged time, it can result in depression.

Depression is the outcome of great sadness or misery taking root in the heart. It can produce conditions capable of hindering the sufferer from enjoying life. One or two days of feeling sadness does not usually result in depression, but when the feeling is allowed to linger for days, weeks, or even months, it opens the doorway to depression. Depression is more than feeling momentarily upset about what has happened to you; it is an illness that leaves you feeling demoralized and often depletes your energy to the point that it becomes hard for you to cope with performing even normal daily activities.

Other negative emotions usually accompany depression, such as fear and anxiety, mental confusion, anguish, and deep sorrow. These are more evident in the lives of those diagnosed with clinical depression. These people may have difficulty dealing with the opinions of others at home or workplace and are susceptible to feeling responsible for everything that has gone wrong in their lives.

Depression is often set off by a combination of things that build up overtime, especially devastating experiences or difficult situations in someone's life. Devastating experiences and hard times can make a person to get into depression state and experiences terrible pain without knowing the source of the pain. A sufferer may feel completely alone or be gripped with fear and not able to tell the reason of being afraid. It can distort their perception of the world and its events to a point that everything seems meaningless and hopeless. One of the most dangerous things about this illness is that an individual with depression can find it difficult to talk about their experiences.

Depression can cause a lot of physical, emotional, and mental problems in the lives of sufferers. They may feel physical pains and aches in their muscles and may find it difficult to get out of bed. There may be times when they go from crying about their experiences to sobbing with such intensity that they become exhausted and feel distraught to the point of collapsing.

Both the young and the old can become depressed. Recent Australian research suggests that around 160,000 young people between the ages of sixteen and twenty-four, and one million adults aged sixteen to eighty-five live with depression each year.[22]

Depression among young people may lead to dropping out of school or quitting their jobs. Depression can wreak havoc in young people's lives and impact their personal, social, and career decisions. When a person becomes depressed, they may feel overwhelmed by the condition and its effects and be at high risk of suicidal thought.

*Kinds of Depression*
Major Depression
Major depression is a mental or behavioural disturbance that affects the normal functioning of the sufferer's emotions and mind, and subjects the sufferer to extensive and continuous low moods. It is also known as clinical, recurrent, or unipolar depression. These names are used particularly to further describe the situation involved with the depression. For example, recurrent depression is used in a situation where the depression is a continual incident or experience. Besides low mood, major depression is often accompanied by low self-image, and loss of interest in the things that a person without depression would usually enjoy.

People with major depression live with disabling conditions that affect their perception and behavioural patterns. They may exhibit some abnormal behaviours towards their family, work, and career. Major depression adversely affects the sleeping and eating habits, and the general health of someone suffering from it. Clinical depression has intense symptoms that may last up to six months or longer, especially when the sufferer is not treated.

*Manic Depression*

---

[22] American Psychiatric Association, ed. ( June 2000) Diagnostic and Statistical Manual of Mental Disorders DSM-IV_TR (4th ed.). American Psychiatric Publishing. ISBN 978-0-89042-024-9

Manic depression, also known as bipolar depression, is a mental or behavioural impairment that affects an individual's normal functioning and ability to feel, act, think, and perceive things in a usual way. It is marked by detectable organic abnormalities of the brain in which major disturbances of the individual's emotions are predominant. There are different phases associated with manic depression which include: hypomanic phase, depressive phase, and mixed affective phase.

The hypomania phase of manic depression is a period of persistently high, broad, or short-tempered mood, lasting for four days or more. This episode is clearly distinct and different from the characteristics and the usual experience that someone with non-depressed mood would have. It is related to an unambiguous change in other experiences that is unusual for the person when the symptoms are not noticeable.

Depressed phase is a period in which a person with manic depression feels as if they are helpless, hopeless, and worthless. It is a phase in which a person with manic depression will look around, and perceive that the happenings around them are senseless, and life seems meaningless. As a result, they may begin to overeat and become less active, which causes them to gain weight. The danger at this point is that they could start to talk about or think about committing suicide.

The depressed phase can be severe, throwing the person with manic depression, into a state of agitation, anxiety, constipation, hypochondria, insomnia, intellectual impairment, physical immobility, delusions, or hallucinations. Mixed affective phase is a period during which a person with manic depression experiences both the symptoms of depression and mania at the same time. The combining effect makes the individual irritable, physically aggressive, and hostile. The overwhelming experience and physical aggressiveness associated with this phase, make it necessary for people in this condition to often be hospitalized for their safety and the safety of people around them.

Manic depression usually causes mood swings that alternate between major depression and mania (an extreme elation). The mood swings can range from mild to extreme, and can occur either gradually or suddenly within a period of time, from minutes to hours. A person with manic depression may have a thinking disorder, distortion of perception, and social functioning impairment.

The cause of manic depression is not yet known, but it has been accepted as a fact that manic depression has a genetic component and environmental risk factors. It is hereditary and can run in families. Manic depression usually appears at a young age, between fourteen and twenty-four years old, and can continue throughout the individual's lifetime. People with severe manic depression may act on their suicidal thoughts. This is why people diagnosed with manic depression are often hospitalized to avoid the risk of them taking their own lives.

*Dysthymia Depression*
Dysthymia depression is a mood disturbance marked by cognitive and physical problems, as in other depressions, but with long lasting and less severe symptoms. It can persist for at least two years for an adult and approximately one year for children and adolescents, according to the Diagnostic and Statistics Manual of Mental Disorders (DSM- IV-TR). It is also known as neurotic or chronic depression.[23]

People with dysthymia may experience symptoms for many years and

---

[23] American Psychiatric Association, ed. (June 2000) Diagnostic and Statistical Manual of Mental Disorders DSM-IV_TR (4th ed.). American Psychiatric Publishing. ISBN 978-0-89042- 024-9

may believe that depression is a part of their character. When this is the case, the sufferer may not seek the help of a physician or discuss their problem with anyone to receive help. They may experience low energy and drive, low self- image, and low capacity for interest in everyday life activities.

Mild dysthymia may cause the sufferer to withdraw from stressful activities and avoid opportunities that could result in failure. In the case of severe dysthymia, the sufferer may even withdraw from day-to-day activities and lose interest in the things from which they usually derive pleasure. Dysthymia can be subtle in nature and difficult to diagnose. This is because a sufferer can hide its symptoms even in social situations. There's a high incidence of one or more additional disorders or illness with dysthymia patients, and suicidal behaviour is a problem for persons with dysthymia.

*Postpartum Depression*
Postpartum depression is a type of depression that can affect women, and less frequently men, after childbirth. Less than 30 per cent of new fathers suffer from postpartum depression. It has debilitating emotional conditions similar to clinical depression and is also called postnatal depression. The causes of postpartum depression are not well understood. Many women who have recovered from postnatal depression did so through support groups and counselling. The symptoms of postpartum depression include a feeling of being overwhelmed and exhausted, the inability to be comforted, sadness, anxiety, irritability, emptiness, hopelessness, sleeping and eating disturbances, a reduced libido, social withdrawal, and crying episodes.
Seasonal Affective Disorder (SAD)

Seasonal Affective Disorder is a mood disturbance in which people who have normal physical, mental, and emotional health during spring and summer, and experience depressive symptoms in autumn and winter. It is also called winter/summer depression or winter/summer blues. Some people experience a serious mood disturbance and change with the season. This disorder may occur at a specific season or time of the year, and during that time it may cause a sufferer to sleep too much, have low energy, and possibly feel depressed. Although the symptoms of Seasonal Affective Disorder can be severe, they usually clear up during spring and summer or autumn and winter as the case may be. People who experience their SAD during spring and summer show the symptoms of insomnia, anxiety, irritability, decreased appetite, weight loss, social withdrawal, and decreased sex drive.

The symptoms of SAD may include difficulty waking up in the morning; nausea; a tendency to oversleep and overeat; a lack of energy; difficulty concentrating on or completing tasks; withdrawal from friends, family, and social activities; and a decrease in sex drive.

*Depression and Anxiety*
Anxiety is a state of uneasiness and apprehension, especially in respect to future uncertainties. It is an emotional state of fear resulting from anticipating a possible danger and fantasizing about threatening situations that may impair one's physical and psychological functioning. Depression and anxiety often go hand in hand, and the presence of one can introduce the other.

When depression and anxiety combine, they usually form a synergy of profound despair, despondency, and misery. When the condition becomes aggravated, the sufferer becomes both overwhelmed and agitated by the experience; therefore, it is harder to treat depression mixed with anxiety. It may require an intense diagnosis and treatment plan—possibly treating each of them separately to achieve the required result. Depression in the presence of anxiety may not be properly treated, because treating depression mixed with anxiety would be like shoveling snow while it is still snowing, or drying your clothes in the rain. It is preferable to treat anxiety first and then the depression; handling both in simultaneously calls for extreme care. It is better to deal with anxiety first, because anxiety has the capacity to act as a stimulant to the conditions of depression. For this reason, it is better to have every trace of anxiety taken away to quicken the recovery process from depression.

It is thought that more than half of depression-related suicides are anxiety driven. When people who have never had a mental illness or any psychological issues in the past suddenly take their lives, the possible cause for their action is depression mixed with anxiety. Anxiety makes the symptoms of depression more severe and may cause increased impairment in the daily lives of the depressed.

*Causes of Depression*
Depression may be caused by one or more factors, including traumatic and difficult experiences in life, stress, genetics, gender, age, health condition, a chemical imbalance in the brain, and substance abuse.

Traumatic experiences in life can cause depression. Everyone feels sad when they lose someone or something they value. A loss through death, however, seems to be the greatest of them all. Bereavement can produce grief and sorrow. It is normal to cry and mourn when we lose a loved one. It is a normal and necessary way to respond to the situation and the feelings it carries. If grief is not harnessed, it may take root in bitterness and anguish, thereby causing great distress to the individual, and it may trigger genuine depression. Not all grief and sorrow over the loss of a loved one will result in depression, but the depth and the breadth of the grief could precipitate it. How long and how deeply someone carries the feelings of great distress determines the possibility of having depression. Trauma comes from the experience of violence—physical or emotional abuse sustained by anyone from childhood or adulthood, which has directly or indirectly influenced their view and attitude towards life. Other factors such as neglect, divorce, or rejection can affect the way someone views the world.

Stress and difficulties in life can also cause depression. Stress is a mentally or emotionally disruptive or upsetting condition that occurs in someone's life in response to adverse external influences. It can affect physical health, potentially causing an increased heart rate, a rise in blood pressure, muscular tension, irritability, and depression. Some physiological reactions to difficulties in life—such as financial difficulties, caring for a sick relative, divorce, living alone, and failure in a career—are factors that can put one at risk of developing depression. Difficult times in life can set off depression by bringing together day-to-day negative interpretations of the experiences and causing them to build up over time. For example, when a worker feels they are doing poorly at their job, when a student feels they are doing badly at school, or when a business person feels their business is not making profits, they become disturbed and stressed. Other possible causes of stress at school or work include being bullied, poor self-esteem, not coping with a situation, not connecting with people, and financial debts.

Genetics, gender, age, and chemical imbalances in the brain are other factors that can cause depression. A family history of depression counts in the diagnosing of depression. Highlights of the First International Conference on Bipolar Disorder (University of Pittsburgh, Pennsylvania, 1994) recognize that depression can run in families as well as racial groups.[24]

---

[24] Bipolar Depression: Highlights of the First International Conference on Bipolar Disorder; University of Pittsburgh, Pennsylvania June 23, 24, 1994

Other researchers have also made similar statements that support this view. This does not necessarily mean that a member of the family must experience depression who has family history in which both or either of the parents have depression. ; However, it does suggest that you have a higher chance of becoming depressed, if depression runs in your family, compared to someone whose family history does not have any traces of depression.

"Researchers believe that chemicals called neurotransmitters are involved in depression. Some of the neurotransmitters believed to be linked to depression are serotonin, norepinephrine, and dopamine."[25] Depression from a chemical imbalance in the brain occurs when part of the brain doesn't seem to be working normally. Studies also show that women are about twice as likely as men to experience depression. It is being guessed that this may be because of the hormonal changes that women experience at different periods in their lives. Individuals, who are advanced in age are prone to depression, because they are often at higher risk of social isolation and loneliness. This may be exceptionally high when they lack the support of friends and family. Individuals who have retired from work and are left uncared for and unsupported, they will start feeling being abandoned and may worry. Anxiety may then set in, which could be followed by depression.

Poor health conditions are another factor that could cause depression. People with chronic illness are at a higher risk of becoming depressed. Illness such as chronic pains, heart disease, head injury, epilepsy, cancer, and many other illnesses (especially persistent and protracted) can increase the risk of depression. Whenever an illness prevails for long duration, it creates a negative feeling in the

---

[25] "The Chemical Connection to Depression" by Bobbie Hasselbring < http://www.howstuffworks.com/mental-health/depression/facts/the-chemical-connection-to-depression. htm >

individual which may lead to depression.

Substance abuse is also a factor that causes depression. Substance abuse is common among people with depression. They are susceptible to the abuse of alcohol, cigarettes, and other drugs, as they often think these things may help them get relief from their conditions. People also abuse prescription drugs, especially when they are too impatient to follow the prescription or the process of recovery. By abusing prescription drugs, chemical imbalances in the brain can be caused that can change bodily functions.

*Emotional Effects of Depression*
Constant feelings of sadness, emptiness, hopelessness, or worthlessness are the emotional effects of depression. When intense feelings of sadness occurring almost every day for no apparent reason, there's no doubt that depression is present. These feelings often suggest that nothing can make them go away. Depression may also be imminent, when someone starts experiencing feelings of guilt for things, they do not have control over. Sometimes a person with depression can feel intense guilt even for minor errors.

Depression can lead to pessimism—a tendency to negative stress, and unfavourable aspects of a situation or life's events. Pessimism is the tendency to expect the worst and see the worst in all things. Depression can make someone irritable or anxious, and short-tempered. Depression can cause restlessness and agitation. For example, depressed persons are unable to sit still and/or keep their hands still. Suicidal thoughts may occur frequently during the period of depression and can vary from person to person. People with depression may wish they were dead, because it would mean an end to their sorrow. Some may also make explicit plans to hurt or end their lives alongside those who they feel are the reason for their situation.

*Psychological Effects of Depression*
Loss of interest, forgetfulness, indecision, or lack of concentration can be symptoms of depression. When you look closely into the life of a depressed person, you will discover that they have lost interest in the things in which they normally take pleasure. The loss of interest in everyday activities which one enjoys, is symptomatic of depression.

People with depression may be affected psychologically, and they may have trouble focusing and making decisions. They may demonstrate a high level of indecision. They may experience a reduced ability to concentrate or think clearly. The effects of depression can be so intense that sufferers feel things have been slowed down in their life, thus decreasing their capacity to think clearly and diminishing their capacity to respond promptly to everyday situations. They may be forgetful and overlook the most important details and information in their life—interviews, exams dates and time, appointments, etc.

*Physical Effects of Depression*
Low energy, aches, pains, weight gain, and weight loss are physical symptoms of depression. The depressed individual's may feel their energy level have lowered, although they have not done any work. This is because depression produces fatigue. Depressive fatigue can disrupt sufferers' sleep patterns. They may become weak, lazy, and tired for no apparent reason. Insomnia or hypersomnia may also set in. They may often wake up in the early hours of the day and experience mental anguish that can prevent them from getting back to sleep—on the other hand, they may be subject to excessive sleeping.

Depression can produce physical aches and pains. People with depression may experience headaches, joint pains, stomach pains, and other physically related pains. Depression can cause psychomotor impairment. Psychomotor impairment is an impairment relating to movement or muscular activities and associated with mental processes or activities. Psychomotor impairment includes physical difficulty in performing activities that normally would require little thought or effort.[26] For example, they may have difficulty in walking up a stairway, getting out of bed, preparing meals, clearing dishes, or returning phone calls. People with depression may gain or lose weight. This is because they may have an increased or decreased appetite for food consumption.

*Identifying Barriers to Recovery from Depression*
There are five barriers to recovery from depression. People with depression are often unaware of the illness and may hide their condition. People with depression may carry the misconception that depression is not treatable, and thereby preventing them from seeking help.

In this respect, ignorance is the number one barrier to recovery from depression. Ignorance of depression, its causes, symptoms, and treatment can be a major roadblock to recovery. Charles Franklin Kettering (August 29, 1876– November 25, 1958), sometimes known as Charles "Boss" Kettering, was an American inventor, engineer, businessman, and the holder of 186 patents. He was a founder of Delco, and was head of research at General Motors from 1920 to 1947. He was one of the most distinguished (and wealthy) engineers of the twentieth century, serving for decades as the director of General Motors' research division.[27] According to Charles Kettering, "A problem well stated is a problem half-solved." However, a problem cannot be well described, specified, or explained when it is not known or acknowledged as a problem. When people with depression are unable to identify and recognize the symptoms of

---

[26] http://www.en.wikipedia.org/wiki/psychomotor_reterdation
[27] https://en.wikipedia.org/wiki/Charles_F._Kettering

depression, it becomes a problem on its own. A lot of people with agonizing pains and the miseries of depression do not even know that they are depressed. Others who know may deny that they are depressed and in turn blame the situation on other people.

A person's past traumatic life experiences can be another barrier to recovery from depression. People who have been abused, bullied, or hurt, and who have repressed feelings of hurt, have a greater chance of becoming depressed. Depressed people who have experienced physical abuse, sexual abuse, emotional abuse, child abuse, break-ups, divorce, and/or family arguments or violence may not seek treatment because they are ashamed to tell others about their abuses.

People suffer and remain in silence when they hide the traumatic events of their lives like abuse, hurt, neglect, divorce, betrayal or denial. A further barrier to recovery occurs when people with depression continue to live in an unsafe or abusive relationship or surround themselves with negative people. In this case, they may find it difficult to be open or talk about their situation, because they fear the ones holding them hostage.

Social isolation is the third barrier to recovery from depression. The recovery process for the depressed can hinder or slow down due to withdrawal from people because of challenging life situations. People who are faced with difficulties in life—unemployment, low income, demanding work, job loss, chronic health conditions—may not like to socialize with other people, including friends and family. They may cease participating in activities and going to social gatherings. They may feel worthless and as a result avoid being among people whom they value more than themselves. They may feel hopeless and choose to remove themselves from people who can encourage, comfort, or advise them on how to get out of their situation. When people with depression remove themselves from people who could help them, it becomes a hindrance in getting the required help.

The fourth barrier to recovery from depression is substance abuse or trying to self-manage depression. When a person with depression decides to self- manage their depression with alcohol or drugs, it becomes a barrier to their recovery. Self-medication and the use of alcohol to treat depression does not cure depression—rather, it leads to further complications. No one can permanently drive away depression, sadness, or sorrow with alcohol. Although the use of these substances may give temporary relief to the symptoms of depression, once the effects are gone, the individual returns to their original situation and most of the time is the worse for wear.

The fifth barrier to recovery from depression occurs when a person with depression is impatient with the treatment procedures, and fails to properly follow through with their prescriptions as recommended. Depression varies and may require different medicines to be tried before a suitable solution is identified. Since it might take time for a doctor to identify the suitable medicine for each individual's condition—and because it takes time for any prescribed drugs to start taking full effect in the individual— patience is absolutely required by the individual with depression. People with depression are also required to stick to their prescription and always communicate any development (positive or negative) in their condition or the treatment to their healthcare professional; otherwise, the chances of a full recovery will be diminished.

*Recovery from Depression*
The good news is that depression is treatable. It is an illness that responds to a variety of treatments. If you suspect you are depressed, do not wait for a long time. Take the signs and symptoms seriously. Begin the journey of getting the right help and try to get it at the earliest. This can make a much easier and faster recovery process.

There are three fundamental factors to recovery from depression, and like the three legs of a stool, each leg is as important as the others. Complete recovery must embrace all three of these factors.

Do not be ashamed or afraid to ask for help. If you suspect or recognize any signs or symptoms of depression, it is important that you see a doctor as soon as possible. The doctor will be able to fully, properly, and accurately diagnose the illness, and identify the kind of depression you are suffering from. It is the healthcare personnel who can prescribe the correct treatment plan for the diagnosed condition. Remember that each medication takes time to show its effects, it becomes your duty to discuss any progress in your condition (or the lack thereof) with your doctor.

Many antidepressants prescribed by healthcare professionals can help a person with depression. Some prescriptions may need other medicines to work better. Remember, sometimes depression can be mixed with anxiety; therefore, proper diagnosis is required to form an effective treatment plan which can be followed. If you have any doubts or questions, discuss them with your doctor.

Depression can be hard to treat unless person with depression fully participate in the recovery, by doing all that is required from them. Firstly, people with depression are required to see medical professionals and discuss their condition. It is important to talk to a healthcare professional, because they have been trained to help people with these conditions. The objective of talking to a doctor about your condition is for them to help you get back your normal life.

Secondly, people with depression are required to follow their prescription accordingly—no abuse, misuse, or disuse. It is not for you, under any circumstances, to make a unilateral change in your treatment plan. You must first talk to your healthcare provider.

Ensure you have a good relationship with your doctor. Be open to discuss your feelings and thoughts about your condition. Thirdly, people with depression are required to have a specific change of lifestyle. As soon as your treatment commences, you can do many things to accelerate your recovery. For example, you can engage in physical exercises that will improve mental and physical health—breathing exercises, muscle relaxation, and fitness exercises. A change in behaviour, nutrition, and getting the required sleep are necessary in stepping up your recovery. It is your responsibility to limit or completely stop alcohol intake and avoid the use of drugs. A person with depression must do all those things which are necessary for the recovery process.

*Social Integration and Support*
People with depression often keep their illness to themselves. They don't usually seek help from friends or family. If they belong to a club, organization, or group, they often remain partially or completely disengaged from the group's activities.

This is why, it is of paramount importance that people with depression seek and ask for help from people close to them. Many suicides can be prevented by family and friends if they know the depth of the situation. Any help from families, friends, or people we trust and respect, can be valuable for the depressed person. Although people with depression often find it difficult to ask for or accept help, when they can summon the courage to do so, they often get valuable support from family and friends. A friend or family member can accompany a depressed person during their visit to clinic or healthcare professional. They can be a great source of encouragement and can constantly check on the person to see how they are doing and keep track of their progress. People with depression should tell about their illness to friends and family who are part of an immediate support system. They can help them better because they understand their illness better. Spend time together with your loved ones and do activities together.

A healthy social life can always help in the recovery of a person with depression. It is important for any depressed person to attend and participate in the social group activities. For example, if your social group is church-based, join either a youth, men's, or women's forum and ensure you partake in your group's programs. When your group goes kayaking, biking, swimming, or to music concerts, and so on, try to participate. By doing so, you'll take away loneliness and boredom, and help your mind and soul relax and be refreshed. Social integration and support can help a person with depression build hope and confidence. If you're involved in spiritual exercises, you can start gaining spiritual healing alongside your physical treatments.

# Chapter Seven:
## The Torment of Guilt and Shame

Adam and Eve had two sons—Cain and Abel. Cain was the firstborn, and he worked on the farm. Abel was the younger son, and he was a shepherd. Both sons of Adam and Eve were asked to offer up individual sacrifice to God. In obedience, each of them presented a sacrifice to God. Cain brought an offering from the produce of his farm. Abel also brought an offering. Abel's offering was the firstborn of his sheep. God liked Abel and his offering, but Cain and his offering didn't get his approval. Cain lost his temper and went into a sulk.

God spoke to Cain: "Why this tantrum? Why the sulking? If you do well, won't you be accepted? And if you don't do well, sin is lying in wait for you, ready to pounce; it's out to get you, you've got to master it." Cain had words with his brother in the field. Cain came at Abel and killed him. God said to Cain, "Where is Abel your brother?" He said, "How should I know? Am I his babysitter?" God said, "What have you done! The voice of your brother's blood is calling to me from the ground."

The story is the same both in the Hebrew Bible and the Qur'an narration. Both books tell the same story that both brothers were asked to make an individual sacrifice—an offering to God. God accepted the sacrifice of Abel, and Cain's sacrifice was rejected. Cain, out of shame and jealousy, killed his brother, Abel. This became the first ever case of murder committed upon the earth.[28]

Cain, perhaps, felt humiliated before his younger brother. The shame that the younger had outperformed the older eroded his feelings. He may have thought about how much respect he would lose from his parents. Shame led to jealousy, and jealousy turned Cain into a murderer. The aftermath was that Cain was full of guilt and shame before God, as God confronted him.

Guilt is a mental as well as an emotional experience that occurs when a person believes or realizes that they have compromised their own standards of conduct or have violated a universal moral standard and takes the responsibility for their action. Shame, which is closely related, is a painful feeling of humiliation or distress caused by the conscious awareness of wrong or foolish behaviour.

*Here's another example:*
Milan Babić, the son of Bozo Babic, was born in the village of Kukar near the town of Vrlika, in SR Croatia, Yugoslavia. In 1981, he graduated from Belgrade University's School of Dentistry. In 1989, he became one of the directors of the medical centre in Knin, a largely Serb-inhabited town in southwestern Croatia. He entered politics in 1990, as Yugoslavia began to disintegrate, leaving the League of Communists of Croatia and joining the newly established nationalist Serbian Democratic Party (SDS) at its inception. He was shortly afterwards elected President of the Municipal Assembly of Knin.

At that time, Serbs comprised about 12.2 per cent of Croatia's population, forming a majority in a strip of land known as "Krajina" along the Croatian-Bosnian border. Croatia's moves towards independence following the election of President Franjo Tuđman,

---
[28] https://en.wikipedia.org/wiki/Cain_and_Abel_in_Islam

were strongly opposed to the partitioning of their country by their Serbian minority, which was supported both politically and militarily by the Yugoslav People's Army ( JNA) and Serbia under President Slobodan Milošević. Nationalist Serbs in "Krajina" established a Serbian National Council to coordinate opposition to Croatia; Babić was elected its president.

Babić was indicted for war crimes by the International Criminal Tribunal for the former Yugoslavia in 2004 and was the first ever indicted to admit guilt. He made a plea bargain with the prosecution, after which he was sentenced to thirteen years in prison. He expressed "shame and remorse" in a public statement and declared that he had acted to relieve the collective shame of the Croatian Serbs. He asked his "Croatian brothers to forgive their Serb brothers" for their actions. He was found dead in his prison cell in The Hague in March 2006, an apparent suicide.[29]

Babić's suicide is an example of the effect of the torment of guilt and shame. He pleaded guilty but it was not the admittance that cost him his life. It was the prolonged torment buried within him after all the wrong things he did.

Guilt is a feeling of being responsible for the commission of an offense. It is accepting moral liability or responsibility for mistakes or errors, whether real or imagined. The feelings of guilt can bother us as much as anxiety would. It can become a huge burden that can tear the soul apart.

Guilt and shame are emotions that relate to our sense of self and our consciousness of others' reactions to or opinion of us. Thus, they are referred to as self-conscious emotions. The development of a sense of self begins to form when we are children and gain the understanding

---

[29] https://en.wikipedia.org/wiki/Milan_Babi%C4%87

that we are different from one another as entities. Moral development emphasizes the relational principle—how individuals ought to behave, and treat one another, and respect rules and regulation. The role of consciousness, values, socialization, and cultural influences are included in the field of moral development, which emerges from infancy through adulthood.

Studies have found that children as young as two to three years of age can express feelings similar to guilt. Even five-year-old children are able to imagine events in which they experience shame or guilt. The capacity to describe vivid events, in which they felt any social emotion does not appear until seven years of age. Self-awareness and self-representation are foundational to self-conscious emotions.

Social emotions such as guilt, shame, embarrassment, empathy, pride, and jealousy are products of self-conscious feelings. What one considers a joke could cause someone else embarrassment. Self-conscious feelings rely on perceptions, thoughts, feelings, or actions of other people as experienced, anticipated recalled, or imagined. Although social emotions are sometime called moral emotions, because of certain roles they play in moral decision- making. They have limitations when the victim is not responsible for what happened. When manipulators, bullies, and haters take on their victim, they can go to any length to achieve their goal. They can use the tool of public shaming or online shaming against their target.

Online shaming is a current and widely used form of public shaming. The use of social and news media to attack and publicly humiliate other people, either by using what they did or twisting what they did. It has become a tool to amass online mobs to destroy the reputation and careers of people or organizations who have made mistakes or unknowingly done something wrong.

Online shaming often involves the viral distribution or publication of private information on the Internet. This is called "doxing" and is the practice of researching and distributing private information about individuals. This method often involves searching publicly available databases and social media websites (like Facebook, Twitter, Instagram, etc.). Online shaming frequently invites and leads to hate messages and even death threats. Victims of doxing may be exposed to cyber-stalking and physical attack.

Negative reviews are another tool for online shaming. Companies often use product reviews from their customers as a means of promoting and improving their products or services, but some products frequently attract negative reviews. In many cases, "reviewers" are people who are either working for a competitor or who out of mere jealousy lash out at companies or authors just because they dislike them.

*How Guilt Affects Us*
Like many things in life, guilt comes in two forms. It is important for us to distinguish between guilt that either comes as a result of an error committed or guilt that comes from the assumption that an error has been committed. True guilt is a feeling of remorse for a deed that by moral and ethical standards is wrong. It is doing something that you feel wrong about and that your conscience condemns.

People, who are aware of how hurtful it can be to offend others or to do things that they would not want others to do to them, are those with a living conscience. Conscience is a built-in check valve that creates the awareness of morality in regards to our behaviour. It is the inward voice that tells us our standing after we have done something good or bad. Conscience urges us to act morally.

True guilt comes from a living conscience. The one that has not been destroyed by repeatedly committing wrongdoings, and the other for which the offender constantly refuses to acknowledge as wrong. For example, people who condemn or punish other people's vices, yet commit the same sins themselves, are people with a dead conscience. Bullies, drug barons, human traffickers, robbers, assassins, etc., are people with a dead conscience. They are people who have silenced their conscience by their constant wrongdoings to the point that they feel nothing after doing wrong. People with a dead conscience feel nothing after doing wrong which people with a living conscience would not dare do.

What about false guilt? False guilt does not imply unreal guilt or artificial feelings of guilt. It is a condition in which someone feels remorse or ashamed for an action, but for which they are not in any way personally responsible. For example, a manager might feel false guilt for firing a longtime employee who is no longer following the company's policies.

People, who grew up seeking attention and who derive their sense of self- worth from other people's approval, have a greater risk of false guilt. They are the people who feel guilty and responsible for their friend's wrongdoing, even they have no connection to the event. They are always the "yes" people. They fear saying "no" to things because they often experience an episode of guilt in the form of regret, when they feel they have failed someone.

Parents often invest time and money on their children education and other activities to raise them for success, despite these children may have troubles, such as addictions, when they become adults. This will hurt the parents, and they might develop false guilty feelings. Whoever makes a choice must prepare to face the consequences of the deed. Parents of adult children who are addicts will likely feel empathy for their children, as well as anxiety. But to empathize is not the same as feeling guilt, because it does not make you responsible for another person's actions.

*How Shame Affects Us*
Next to the torment of guilt is the torment of shame. Shame is a painful feeling of humiliation or distress caused by the awareness of having done something wrong. It is the conscious awareness of wrong or foolish behaviour that one experiences when a regrettable or unfortunate event happens. Since shame is closely related to guilt, we often mistake one for the other. When they get mixed up, it becomes difficult to get a positive outcome for the individual involved.

Whereas guilt is concerned with the deed, shame is concerned with the doer. Shame takes focus off what someone did and puts the spotlight on the personality of the person who did the wrong. Shame is the feeling of disappointment about who you are, or about how and what you did will define you. It affects your thinking and takes a toll on your self-perception.

The torment of shame is stronger than guilt. Shame keeps you on the hook and puts emphasis on your perceived weaknesses, inadequacies, and inferiority. Shame swallows a person's good nature and all the good deed they have done. It pulls all their past mistakes and failures from the inward parts of their life and blows up and magnifies their weaknesses to the point that they see nothing but their inability to make right their wrongdoings.

There exists the difference between guilt and shame, it is important to understand how to differentiate one from another. The imperfection in us can lead us to make mistakes and errors. While we might feel guilty and take responsibility for our mistakes, we should not let this develop into the heightened pain and destructive feelings of shame and inadequacy. The awareness of right and wrong, in regards to what is morally acceptable and ethically right associated with guilt, is proof that we are continuously striving for perfection.

Guilt is connected to responsibility and accountability. It points out what you did wrong and convinces you to be accountable for it. But shame brings you down, and it may convince you to blame other people for your errors. The pain of shame makes you to find temporary relief, and it can blind you from acknowledging the wrong deed.

Shame is the primary reason why we blame others for our self-induced failures. The act of dodging responsibility and shifting it around does not help to fix the problems. Shame blames everyone—parents, friends, and colleagues. Guilt feels bad but becomes better when there is a turnaround. We can all embrace change that comes from realizing we did something wrong and making sure we never repeat the same mistake. Shame is the chief architect of blame and the foundation for stagnation in life. It keeps pointing fingers and ignoring the root cause of what has happened.

People, who are overcome by their shame, are more likely to pursue their freedom and redeem their name through pursuing perfection, popularity, power, or fame. This process does not remove the deed but may temporarily cover it. The attempt to cover up shame rather than completely removing it, can result in the repetition of the same mistake if the opportunity ever comes again. Cover-up and pretense are not the options to freedom from tormenting emotions.

If you have fallen into shame, you may also experience self-denial. This is the sacrifice of one's personal interests or wellbeing for the sake of other people. The masking of shame by being nice can sometimes be disastrous. Any attempt to compensate shame by being overly kind at the expense of what is right, does not better a person.

In fact, you may get into more trouble by becoming over-committed, your life becomes stressed and you may start breaking down inwardly.

Shame is also fundamental to isolation. People who isolate themselves from contemporaries often do so because of shame. The fear of failing and the aftermath of failure can introduce shame, which attacks the personality of the individual. For example, if James thinks he is better than John, but after several attempts has failed to achieve the same things that John has, he may become preoccupied with the shame of failure and withdraw from John and other friends.

When shame has convinced an individual to withdraw, it introduces them to destructive vices such as substance abuse and/or depression, because shame attacks one's self-image. It can prevent us from the changes for the better. It makes us focus on what we don't like about ourselves and how other people are better than us. Shame locks us up in the prison of "self- inadequacies."

People with shame and who have withdrawn themselves from others are likely to eat too much and become overweight. Shame will also prevent them from going to the gym due to fear that they may embarrass themselves at the fitness center. Shame also prevents people from talking about their problems. It prevents people from connecting with people who could help them.

In addition to the "blame game," being defensive is another tool of shame. When someone says, "It's not my fault," instead of taking responsibility for their actions, they are beginning to walk down the path of denial. This is because they have internalized the impact of their shame, and it has impacted their sense of who they are. They are constantly haunted by poor self-image. It gives shame more footholds by becoming defensive which endangers the individual under its grip.

When we realize the difference between guilt and shame, and choose to be accountable for the choices we make in life, we can manage our life experiences in a healthy way. Handling humiliation and embarrassment wisely, and building our confidence through knowledge are vital in overcoming the torment of guilt and shame. While guilt can produce positive change, false guilt can make people take responsibility and blame themselves for things which they are not in any way responsible. Confessing your problems and fighting these feelings can lead the way to internal freedom.

# Chapter Eight:
## The Agony of Abandonment

Countless people everywhere in the world experience abandonment—some from parents, a spouse, siblings, or relatives. The alarming rate of break-ups in relationships and the statistics of divorce are proving that many people's lives are being shaped by negative experiences. These experiences can affect perception and attitude and, therefore, shape the lives of people who have been abandoned.

Abandonment is the act of giving up or discontinuing any further interest in someone or something because of discouragement, weariness, loss of interest, or damaged emotions. Abandonment exists in two forms—physical and emotional.

Physical abandonment is the visible or bodily act of intentionally and permanently deserting one's spouse and/or children, including emotionally and any form of unwanted separation through divorce or death. Physical abandonment is evident in separation, divorce, death, parents leaving a child, children leaving their parents, desertion by friends. Emotional abandonment is withdrawal, unavailability of parents, cold or distant parents, verbal abuse, and cheating.

Parents that withhold nurturing, stimulation, and support from their children are emotionally abandoning them. Spouses who have lost affection for each other, and stopped open communication and support have emotionally abandoned their relationship—either directly or indirectly. They have both shut the other out and emotionally withdrawn from the relationship. Emotional abandonment often precedes physical abandonment. Many spouses are physically present in a relationship but have emotionally left their marriage many years ago. They are emotionally separated from their spouse, even though they may live together. Apart from existing relationships, people who feel undesired, left behind, insecure, or discarded are liable to live in a state of emotional abandonment.

Child abandonment can lead to Abandoned Child Syndrome—a behavioural or psychological condition that remains throughout the child's life. Abandoned Child Syndrome is not recognized as a mental disorder in any medical manuals, but its psychological damage to the child cannot be denied. When a child is raised with chronic loss, or in an extremely dysfunctional relationship without the emotional supports and protection they need and certainly deserve, they are highly likely to internalize those experiences, which in turn can damage their perception of self and life.

An Alex Greig article published by the Associated Press on May 24, 2014 shared a devastating story of the agony of abandonment. The following is the story as posted on the dailymail.co.uk and Associated Press website.

On May 23, 2014, at about 9:30 p.m. in Isla Vista near the University of California, Santa Barbara Elliot Rodger, who has reached a breaking point in his agony of abandonment went on a drive by shooting rampage that killed six people and injured fourteen others near a student enclave.

Prior to the incident, he posted on social media called "Elliot Rodger's Retribution"—in which he rants about women who supposedly rejected his advances. Elliot Rodger unleashes a tirade about his "loneliness, rejection, and unfulfilled desires," blaming women for preferring "obnoxious brutes" to him, "the supreme gentleman".

"I'm 22 years old, and I'm still a virgin. I've never even kissed a girl," he says in the video. "College is the time when everyone experiences those things such as sex and fun and pleasure. But in those years, I've had to rot in loneliness. It's not fair. You girls have never been attracted to me. I don't know why you girls aren't attracted to me. But I will punish you all for it," he says in the video, which runs to almost seven minutes. He promises to "punish" women and lays out a "retribution" plan.

"I'm going to enter the hottest sorority house of UCSB, and I will slaughter every single spoilt, stuck-up, blonde s*** that I see inside there," he says. "All those girls that I've desired so much, they would have all rejected me and looked down on me as an inferior man if I ever made a sexual advance towards them. I'll take great pleasure in slaughtering all of you. You will finally see that I am, in truth, the superior one. The true alpha male.

"Yes... After I have annihilated every single girl in the sorority house I will take to the streets of Isla Vista and slay every single person I see there. All those popular kids who live such lives of hedonistic pleasure..." His YouTube account contains numerous other videos in which Rodger talks of his loneliness and anger at the women he says snub him.

Rodger's Twitter account has only two tweets, posted on April 19 and 20.

"Why are girls sexually attracted to obnoxious, brutish men instead of sophisticated gentlemen such as myself? #girls #perverted #sex

#unfair," reads the first. "Why do girls hate me so much?" he posted on April 20, along with a now-deleted YouTube video.[30]

Rodger was the son of Peter Rodger, assistant director of the Hollywood film franchise The Hunger Games. Rodger is an example of someone who felt emotionally isolated and/or abandoned. He did not share his emotional anguish with anyone, but instead he repressed those feelings until they exploded, leading him to make an unthinkable decision.[31]

Emotional abandonment is a subjective emotional state that includes the feelings of disconnection, fear of a future breakup, lack and absence of communication, betrayal, and self-sabotage. Emotional erosion is a gradual process of being absolutely cut off from a crucial emotional tie and the sustenance of a relationship.

The emotional injuries and the pains that follow abandonment can make it a devastating experience. It is capable of creating mental disorders as well as behavioural problems. When people are abandoned, they suffer deep wounds that may remain unless something better replaces them or the victim works themselves through the healing process. The following examples are some possible effects of unmanaged devastation inflicted by abandonment.

Kate Aurthur's post about Danny Bonaduce, entitled "An Excruciating Excess of Reality," appeared on September 4, 2005 on nytimes.com. Kate wrote:

During a scene in the fifth episode of VH1's new reality series Breaking Bonaduce, Danny Bonaduce, the former child star from The

---

[30] http://www.dailymail.co.uk/news/article-2638049/7-dead-drive-shooting-near-UC-Santa- Barbara.html

[31] https://en.wikipedia.org/wiki/2014_Isla_Vista_killings#Perpetrator

Partridge Family, is playing with his 10-year-old daughter, Isabella. "Daddy, what happened to your wrists?" she asks, looking at the bandage he was wearing. As she swings in and out of the frame, Mr. Bonaduce lies to her. "Oh, it's nothing," he says with a slight grimace. "Daddy's just not a very handy guy when it comes to installing windows."

What actually happened to Mr. Bonaduce's wrists is that he slashed them after his wife, Gretchen, asked him for a divorce. It was the last desperate act in a long, crazy night that started with hours of drinking and taking pills, and it landed him in the psychiatric ward.

When relationships fail, human emotional attachments are traumatized. The ability to make good decisions can be impaired, and the person involved may take drastic measures to exit the overwhelming experience. The reason why the loss of someone (or something) we value wounds so deeply is all about an emotional-tie that is sometimes called a soul-tie. You may ask, "Why is a soul-tie always associated with emotion?" We are emotional beings and emotions are a part of the human soul. They are designed to control and direct the course of our lives and determine how we will respond or react to our life experiences. Some emotions can be more dominant than others.

When we allow our emotions to dominate or pass through a repeated cycle through exposure to a particular act, place, person, or object, it causes an attachment, or tie, to be formed. Over a period of time, as the cycle goes on and on, it subconsciously starts to affect and control our mind and direct the course of our life.

Feelings are powerful and they are capable of making any individual to take bold action to achieve something great. Negative emotions can compel people to do something extremely dangerous without fear or regard to restrictions, and/ or the consequences for their action could result.

It hurts so deeply when strong bonds (especially those of a relationship) are broken without notice. When bonds are broken without emotional preparation to withstand the shock, it can cause mental devastation. The most effective way to protect oneself and relationships from both physical and emotional abandonment is to avoid those destructive actions that destroy relationships—criticism, blame, nagging, yelling, complaining, manipulating, the silent treatment, sarcasm, and threats.

A flourishing relationship is characterized by love, faithfulness, and trust. Couples that have a good understanding of finance, practice open communication, make time for romance, complement each other, are considerate of each other, do exciting and fun things together, respect each other's interests, and resolve conflict without much delay usually experience overflowing affection for each other.

People with physical and/or emotional abandonment issues can still find help and hope. They can experience freedom from the pain and be restored emotionally.

*How to Handle Loss*

Abandonment is a form of loss. It is usually accompanied by feelings of emptiness, grief, and anger. Every loss produces some ill effect that can demoralize, inject fear and anxiety, and lead to depression, suicidal thoughts, and suicide. The following information and guide can help people who are grieving over a loss or in agony of abandonment to develop resilience, persevere, and hope to pursue their dream without the past holding them down. Here are keys to handling loss due to abandonment or any form of loss that we experience in life.

Acknowledge and don't be in denial: To accept the existence and truth of the fact that something has happened to you and hurt your feelings is fundamental to a quick recovery. When you are dying inwardly, denial and pretending to be strong will not help rid you of your pain. When you fail or experience abandonment in a relationship, do not bury your feelings of hurt, anger, and grief, but face the reality of what has happened and truly admit how you feel about it.

Do not block your grieving: It is normal and common to experience hurt in your life so always accept the hurt and grieve about it. By grieving you can express various emotions within your soul such as anger, guilt, grief, hatred—all of which you need to recognize in order to open the door for your healing. The statement "Men don't cry" is a falsehood. "Big ladies don't care" is another one. It is wrong if someone suggests you sweep what has happened under the carpet. Never repress your emotions, and don't hide or bury them.

Realize that failure or loss is never final: Failure or loss is never final. The lessons learned from failure can reveal what we are doing is different than what we should be doing, or what we are failing to do. People who have undergone several divorces can pause and look inward. Self-examination is the way to go in the case of multiple breakups. Children, who were unfortunate enough to be abandoned by parents, can seek out help or get a mentor or someone who can give them love, support, and encouragement, perhaps as an imaginary father figure in their lives.

People who have destroyed their lives because of what they have lost never get to live again. Just as the saying goes, "Two wrongs do not make a right." Two deaths cannot compensate for the sorrow and grief that goes with loss in life and relationships. Adult children who are mourning the loss of their parents should realize that their parents mourned the same way for their own parents. It is like a cycle. When the call comes, someone must answer.

Choose to forgive: This is probably the toughest thing to ask when someone has hurt you. The truth is that forgiveness brings freedom to both parties. People remain bound to the past by choosing not to forgive. Negative feelings from past experiences, in the absence of forgiveness, may sneak into future relationships. A lack of forgiveness creates unhappiness irrespective of how good a new relationship may be. The pain of the past can mar the stability of your joy. Little things could cause you to snap and take the anger of your past experiences out on your new partner.

What lesson can one learn from abandonment? What positive feeling can emerge from being broken? The likely products of abandonment are sadness, hatred, pain, anger, and fear. Forgiveness is difficult to embrace by those who have been abandoned; therefore, the pain of abandonment tends to stay alive and buried both in the subconscious and unconscious mind.

Anyone who has been abandoned should look out for the pain it can cause. It could remain buried in the heart, and indirectly control thoughts and behaviour. It hurts deeply, but the cure for the agony is to embrace forgiveness. When we acknowledge that life is a gift and there is nothing more valuable than being alive, we will work hard not to cut our lives short. Forgiveness is a valuable tool for sustaining life.

Perform soul-searching: Soul-searching is a deep and anxious consideration of one's emotions and motives. It is the careful consideration of the correctness of one's course of action. It is highly recommended that people, who have experienced multiple rejections in relationships, search out their motives and how they may have expressed them. Next to soul-searching is considering one's personality. The combination of one's characteristics or qualities that form their individual distinctive character is referred to as personality. A good personality is attractive. Take the time to look inward and see if you have a character problem. Fix your character and develop caring as an attribute. These qualities will not only attract the right people into your life, but they also will help you sustain your relationships.

Partake and participate in a support group: It is highly advisable for anyone, who needs to escape the grip of hurt, anger, and grief, to get into a support group. A support group is a group of people with common experiences or concerns, who provide each other with encouragement, comfort, and advice. We need to work with people who can support us to achieve success and have good relationships. We aren't wired to make it alone. We need people to connect with for acceptance, support, motivation, encouragement, advice, guidance, etc. We need to share our feelings with people who will not be judgmental, and who will accept us for who we are.

# Chapter Nine:
## The Deceptions of Suicidal Thoughts

According to the World Health Organization (WHO), about 800,000 people die due to suicide every year, and there are many more who attempt suicide. A previous suicide attempt is the biggest risk factor for suicide. Millions of people in our world today are affected by or experience bereavement every year. "Suicide occurs throughout the lifespan and was the second leading cause of death among youth aged 15-29 years globally in 2012," according to WHO. A study has shown that suicide is a global phenomenon in all regions of the world. In fact, 75 per cent of global suicides occurred in low-and middle-income countries in 2012. Suicide accounted for 1.4 per cent of all deaths worldwide, making it the fifteenth leading cause of death in 2012.[32] Researchers have found that there are twenty hidden failed attempts for each suicide that is successfully carried out.

Here's an important question: Why do so many people attempt suicide every year? In 2015, I sought an answer to this question from a colleague. I chose to talk to Cliff because he was sixty-four years old and had experienced life. Cliff, who is both a good narrator as well as good listener, was surprised when I asked him, "Why do people commit suicide?"

He shared his personal experiences with me, and we talked about

---

[32] http://www.who.int/mental_health/prevention/suicide/suicideprevent/en/

issues like hardship, stress, failure, and frustration. He then said to me, "I think people make the choice to end their life when they have reached their breaking point." That hit me. I then had a flashback to what I had been taught in school. It is called "Hooke's Law."

Hooke talked about the "breaking point" in his law, but he used the term "deformation" to describe what happens when a material exceeds its elasticity and has reached the point that it can no longer return to its regular form. This is what Cliff called the "point of no return."

Suicidal thoughts begin when people reach the point where they become overwhelmed and stressed with their problems, they begin to think it would be better to end their life. It begins with a frustration that won't go away, a debt that won't get paid, a marriage that is not working, or a business that will not grow, and the feelings of abandonment, guilt, shame, harassment, etc. that go with these kinds of problems.

The point of no return happens when pain, hurts, disappointment, and rejection get accumulated. This leads to worry, anxiety, depression, and ultimately, suicidal thoughts. Rich people can have as many worries as the poor. The truth is that people do not want to die except when they think it is the best option for them in their predicament. "It is not that I want to die … it just hurts too much to live," read one suicidal note.

The action of killing oneself intentionally can be caused by factors to which many of us rarely pay attention. It's not an easy or desirable decision for those who consider suicide; these are people who feel drowned in the ocean of their experiences and have lost any hope of surviving their predicaments.

*Factors in Suicide*

The following are the ten top factors that influence people to commit suicide:

*Depression:* Anyone can experience depression in their lifetime. Depression carries with it a sense of hopelessness, helplessness, and worthlessness. When people are depressed, they can be subjected to suicidal thoughts because of the ongoing, relentless trauma they are experiencing. A large percentage of suicides happens because something bad happened and the victim was overwhelmed and could not handle it. This overwhelming negative emotion produces fear and anxiety, and eventually, depression.

Depression, when untreated, can multiply the pain and anguish until it ends in suicide. An example of this occurred on May 19, 1931, when Ralph Barton shot himself through the right temple in his East Midtown Manhattan penthouse apartment. He was thirty-nine years old. Ralph Barton (August 14, 1891–May 19, 1931) was an American artist best known for his cartoons and caricatures of actors and other celebrities. His suicide note said he had irrevocably "lost the only woman I ever loved" (ex-wife Carlotta Monterey, the actress who had divorced Barton in 1926 and married Eugene O'Neill in 1929), and that he feared his worsening manic-depression was approaching insanity.[33]

*Great Loss*: Every one of us has at one point or another lost something. It could be as little as five cents or as large as thousands of dollars. Someone may have lost something even more valuable, such as loved ones. When it comes to material things, what one considers a great loss may not be what another considers as such. It all depends on perception and values. Great loss can compel people who have lost hope of bouncing back to commit suicide.

For example: Edwin Howard Armstrong (December 18, 1890–

---

[33] http://www.en.wikipedia/wiki/Ralph_Barton#Death

January 31, 1954) was an American electric engineer and inventor, best known for developing the FM (frequency modulation) radio. He held forty-two patents and received numerous awards, including the first Medal of Honor awarded by the Institute of Radio Engineers (now IEEE), the French Legion of Honor, the 1941 Franklin Medal, and the 1942 Edison Medal.

Armstrong lashed out at his wife one day with a fireplace poker, striking her on the arm, due to mounting financial problems. She left their apartment to stay with her sister, Marjorie Tuttle, in Granby, Connecticut.

Sometime during the night of January 31/February 1, 1954, Armstrong removed the air conditioner from a window in his twelve-room apartment on the thirteenth-floor of River House in Manhattan, New York City, and jumped to his death. His body fully clothed, with a hat, overcoat, and gloves—was found in the morning on a third-floor balcony by a River House employee. The New York Times described the contents of his two-page suicide note to his wife: "He was heartbroken at being unable to see her once again, and expressing deep regret at having hurt her, the dearest thing in his life." The note concluded, "God keep you and Lord have mercy on my Soul."[34]

*Terminal Illness*: Chronic disease and illness are agents of suicidal thoughts, especially in the absence of hope for survival. The word "terminal" sounds the same as the word "terminate" to anyone in such a condition. Seriously ill people often think they are wasting resources and putting stress on their loved ones, and by ending their life would put a stop to this. Terminal illness results in a large number of suicides committed around the world—some of which are assisted.

For example: Forrest Anderson, former Governor of Montana, killed

---

[34] https://en.wikipedia.org/wiki/Edwin_Howard_Armstrong#Death

himself at seventy-six. His death was ruled a suicide by the coroner, who said Mr. Anderson had shot himself in the abdomen. Gene Daly, a former State Supreme Court Justice, who was a longtime friend, said: "I would think he just got damn tired of being sick. I know he was unhappy about being incapacitated."[35]

*Confusion*: Confusion is a state in which people are uncertain about what to do or unable to understand something clearly. These are feelings people experience when they cannot understand what is happening in their life or career. A confused person can feel helpless and at the same time lack the courage to ask for help—probably because they do not know who to ask or how to begin. Prolonged confusion can carry alongside it the feeling of being isolated or the desire to isolate oneself from other people. This isolation provides an opportunity for suicidal thoughts, and later the act of suicide.

*A Difficult Situation*: The difficult and overwhelmed situations can generate suicidal thoughts in any individual. When people are faced with difficult circumstances, and despite their best efforts nothing changes, they may experience suicidal thoughts. If the frustration they are faced with seems insurmountable and they feel pressured, they could think the quickest option for an escape is to end their life. Suicide is a difficult decision for anyone to make, but when external forces overpowers the internal forces, it is likely that an undisciplined mind will consider it.

An example of this is Jason Altom (1971–1998), a Ph.D. student who was working in the research group of Nobel laureate Elias James Corey at Harvard University. He killed himself by taking potassium

---

[35] "Forrest Anderson, Ex-Governor Of Montana, Kills Himself at 76" by AP Published: July 23, 1989 <http://www.nytimes.com/1989/07/23/obituaries/forrest-anderson-ex-governor-of- montana-kills-himself-at-76.html>

cyanide in 1998, citing in his note "abusive research supervisors" as one reason for taking his life. Altom was studying a complex natural product and felt enormous pressure to finish the molecules before starting his academic career.[36]

*Boredom*: When people no longer find life interesting and have absolutely nothing to do or consider no purpose of life, they feel like life is meaningless and there is no point to wait idly. The lack of inspiration, ambition, goals, and interest in the world for such individuals is a good reason for suicide.

Consider George Sanders. George Henry Sanders (3 July 1906–25 April 1972) was an English film and television actor, singer-songwriter, music composer, and author. His career as an actor spanned more than forty years. His upper- class English accent and bass voice often led him to be cast as sophisticated but villainous characters. He was a man who had everything: four wives (including Zsa Zsa and her sister Magda) over the years, seven psychiatrists, more than ninety film appearances, and an Oscar. But all that wasn't enough to keep him interested. In 1972, at age sixty-five, Sanders swallowed five bottles of Nembutal in a hotel room in Castelldefels, Spain, and took his final curtain. He left a legacy in the form of his suicide note: When the message had made headlines, the world knew it had a classic farewell on its hands. "Dear World," Sanders wrote in part, "I am leaving because I am bored."[37]

*Substance Abuse*: The abuse of drugs and alcohol can mentally affect one's life and gradually lead to a disorder. Substance abuse can cause euphoria, intoxication, ecstasy, and/or depression when done in excess. It can slow a user's breathing, increase heart rate, and cause sedative hypnotism, according to medical findings. People who abuse

---

[36] http://en.wikipedia.org/wiki/Jason_Altom
[37] https://en.wikipedia.org/wiki/George_Sanders

substances can experience heightened depression leading to suicidal thoughts and thus suicide. It is better to confront our challenges than to wish them away with drugs or alcohol.

For example: William Stuart Adamson (11 April 1958–16 December 2001) was a Scottish guitarist, vocalist, and songwriter. He was the co-founder, lead vocalist, and guitarist of the rock group Big Country, which rose to prominence in 1983. Prior to that, he founded the Scottish art-punk band Skids. In the 1990s, he founded the alternative country rock act 'The Raphaels.'

On 26 November 2001, Adamson was reported missing by his wife, Melanie. At the time, the couple had been estranged for six weeks, and Melanie had filed for divorce on the day of his disappearance. Adamson was due to face drunk-driving charges in March 2002 and was ordered to attend Alcoholics Anonymous. He was an alcoholic and resumed drinking after being sober for over a decade. On 16 December 2001, his body was found in a closet in his room at the Best Western Plaza Hotel in Honolulu, Hawaii. According to police, Adamson hanged himself with an electrical cord from a pole in the wardrobe. An empty wine bottle was found in the room. At the time of his death, Adamson had a blood-alcohol content of 0.279 per cent.[38]

*Self-blame:* A guilty conscience is the feeling experienced by someone who is aware of having done something wrong. It is the remorse caused by feeling responsible for some offense. People who derive pleasure and depend on people for personal affirmation can be subjected to remorse and self-blame if they disappoint someone. When this becomes the case, the person may resort to suicide.

An example of this was the Albert Ayler case. Albert Ayler ( July 13,

---

[38] https://en.wikipedia.org/wiki/Stuart_Adamson

1936– November 25, 1970) was an American avant-garde jazz saxophonist, singer, and composer. Born in Cleveland, Ohio, Ayler was first taught alto saxophone by his father, Edward, who was a semi-professional saxophonist and violinist. Edward and Albert played alto saxophone duets in church and often listened to jazz records together, including swing era jazz and then-new bop albums. Ayler's upbringing in the church had a great impact on his life and music, and much of his music can be understood as an attempt to express his spirituality, including the aptly titled "Spiritual Unity," and his album of spirituals, Goin' Home, which features "meandering" solos that are meant to be treated as meditations on sacred texts, and at some points as "speaking in tongues" with his saxophone.[39]

Mary Parks (his girlfriend and known professionally as Mary Maria) told her version of the death of Albert Ayler to English discographer Mike Hames in 1983. She said, "The strains of surviving as a musician in New York seriously affected the mind of Albert's brother, Donald. Their mother (Myrtle Ayler) blamed Albert for introducing Donald to the musician's life and continually pressed Albert to look after Donald." But Donald's increasingly erratic behaviour fuelled by heavy drinking, was inching toward what would later be described as a nervous breakdown, and in 1968 he was gone from the band.

As the decade wound down, Albert was suffering from a tremendous amount of guilt about his brother's unstable condition. His mother had not wanted Donald to move to New York, and now that he was unable to care for himself, she insisted that Albert step up. Albert and Mary wanted Donald to return to Cleveland to be looked after at home. The rift in the family was causing an increasing amount of strain. Albert was trying for a quieter life and he moved out of

---

[39] https://en.wikipedia.org/wiki/Albert_Ayler

Manhattan to live with Mary in an apartment in Park Slope, Brooklyn. The night he disappeared, Ayler again told his lover, "My blood has got to be shed to save my mother and my brother." He smashed one of his saxophones over their television set and stormed out of the house. Mary called the police to report Albert missing.[40]

He disappeared on November 5, 1970 and was found in New York City's East River on November 25, a presumed suicide. For some time afterwards, rumours circulated that Ayler had been murdered. Later, however, Parks would say that Ayler had been depressed and feeling guilty, blaming himself for his brother's problems.[41]

*Bullying, Embarrassment, and Scandal*: A publicized incident that brings about disgrace or offends the moral sensibilities of a person or group can bring suicidal thoughts to the victim(s). Any damage done to someone's reputation by public disclosure of his or her immoral or grossly improper behaviour may result in suicide.

John Clifford "Cliff" Baxter (September 27, 1958 – January 25, 2002) was a former Enron Corporation executive who resigned in May 2001 before committing suicide the following year. Prior to his death he had agreed to testify before Congress in the case of Enron.

Enron Corporation was an American energy company based in Houston, Texas. Enron was formed in 1985 by Kenneth Lay after merging Houston Natural Gas and InterNorth. Several years later, when Jeffrey Skilling was hired, he developed a staff of executives that were able to hide billions of dollars in debt from failed deals and projects by the use of accounting loopholes, special purpose entities, and poor financial reporting. Chief Financial Officer Andrew Fastow

---

[40] http://www.organissimo.org/forum/index.php?/topic/28100-mary-mariamary-parks-albert- ayler
[41] https://en.wikipedia.org/wiki/Albert_Ayler

and other executives not only misled Enron's board of directors and audit committee on high-risk accounting practices, but also pressured Arthur Andersen to ignore the issues. Enron's complex financial statements were confusing to shareholders and analysts. In addition, its complex business model and unethical practices required that the company use accounting limitations to misrepresent earnings and modify the balance sheet to indicate favorable performance.[42]

The Enron scandal, publicized in October 2001, eventually led to the bankruptcy of the Enron Corporation, an American energy company based in Houston, Texas, and the de facto dissolution of Arthur Andersen, which was one of the five largest audit and accountancy partnerships in the world. In addition to being the largest bankruptcy reorganization in American history at that time, Enron was cited as the biggest audit failure.

Most of the top executives were tried for fraud after it was revealed in November 2001 that Enron's earnings had been overstated by several hundred million dollars.[43] Clifford Baxter was found dead in his black Mercedes-Benz in Sugar Land, Texas, with a gunshot wound through the right side of his head. An autopsy was performed by the coroner, and the death was ruled a suicide.

His suicide note was hand printed, though not signed, for his wife, Carol. The letter expressed Baxter's despair over the direction his life had taken.

The full text of the note read:

*Carol,*

---

[42] https://en.wikipedia.org/wiki/J._Clifford_Baxter
[43] "Enron Fast Facts" from CNN Library; Updated 3:39 PM ET, Thu April 27, 2017<http://www.cnn.com/2013/07/02/us/enron-fast-facts/index.html>

*I am so sorry for this. I feel I just can't go on. I have always tried to do the right thing but where there was once great pride now it's gone. I love you and the children so much. I just can't be any good to you or myself. The pain is overwhelming.*

*Please try to forgive me. Cliff*

He was survived by his wife and two children—a son and a daughter.[44]

*Religion and Philosophical Desire*: The ideology of martyrdom and philosophical desire can make one willingly choose to commit suicide.

People's philosophy in life and faith in religion are so powerful that they can influence their desires. They can compel them to commit suicide to protect their pride or faith. Suicide influenced by religious or other beliefs or misconceptions can come in the form of suicide bombers, familicide, mass suicides, etc. Here is an example

For example: Hans Wilhelm Langsdorff (20 March 1894–20 December 1939) was a German naval officer, most famous for his command of the panzerschiff (pocket battleship) Admiral Graf Spee during the Battle of the River Plate. He held the rank of Kapitän zur (naval captain).

Langsdorff's luck ran out on the morning of 13 December 1939 when his lookouts reported sighting a British cruiser and two destroyers. Admiral Graf Spee now suffered engine fatigue that reduced her top speed to 23kn. After Langsdorff had committed his ship to the attack, it became apparent that the destroyers were in fact light cruisers (HMS Ajax and HMNZS Achilles), in addition to the heavy cruiser

---

[44] https://en.wikipedia.org/wiki/Enron_scandal#Causes_of_downfall

HMS Exeter. Naval analysts claim that Langsdorff then committed a grievous tactical error.

Langsdorff learned that he had sixteen hours of pre-cleaned fuel in his ready tanks—with no hope of replacement or repairs to the system at sea. Soon, the two light cruisers got into range and scored twenty hits on Admiral Graf Spee, including the food stores and bakeries. Simultaneously, Langsdorff and the British commodore decided to break off the action, Langsdorff heading for the neutral port of Montevideo in Uruguay to make repairs.

The Uruguayan authorities followed international treaties and, although granting an extra seventy-two hours stay over the normal twenty-four hours, required that Admiral Graf Spee leave port by 20:00 on 17 December 1939 or else be interned for the duration of the war. Langsdorff sought orders from Berlin, and was given instructions that the ship was not to be interned in Uruguay (which was sympathetic to Britain), or to be allowed to fall into enemy hands, but he was given no directive as to what action to take. He therefore considered that he could try to take the ship to the friendlier Buenos Aires in Argentina (Buenos Aires is the capital and most populous city of Argentina).

In Argentina, Langsdorff was taken to the Naval Hotel in Buenos Aires, where he wrote letters to his family and superiors. He wrote on December 19, 1939: "I can now only prove by my death that the fighting services of the Third Reich are ready to die for the honour of the flag. I alone bear the responsibility for scuttling the panzerschiff (armored ship) Admiral Graf Spee. I am happy to pay with my life for any possible reflection on the honour of the flag. I shall face my fate with firm faith in the cause and the future of the nation and of my Führer." Langsdorff then lay on Admiral Graf Spee's battle ensign and shot himself, forestalling any allegations that he had avoided further action through cowardice.[45]

*Debunking the Lies of Suicidal Thoughts*
*Lying thought #1*: "I am doomed or permanently stuck." While it is true that unpleasant circumstances can be distressing and as a result make the persons who find themselves in the situation worry about or fear the worst, it is not factual that they are doomed. Just think of any worst-case situation and research if anyone has been into it and come out victorious, and you will discover that people do come out of "hell" (terrible and unimaginable situations) alive. In some cases, the discipline and skills they acquire during hard times often make them great and successful in life. Those who are drowned by their experience and who believed that they are doomed are usually the people that end their lives in ignorance.

*Lying thought #2*: "I can't handle it." People who think of taking their lives often assume they can't handle their situation any longer, but the opposite is usually the case. There is no situation that comes to anyone that can't be handled. The problem is that when we don't seek out the tools to handle the situation, we become so clouded by the problem that we can't see any solution. Take, for instance, winter cold. Sometimes during winter in certain parts of the country, the pile of snow can be so high that it almost reaches the height of the lintel of houses, but humans living in those areas still survive to next winter. When you have tools, you can handle tough situations. The problem is many people die before their circumstances swallow them up.

*Lying thought #3*: "I am the only one in this." This is not true. There is no road you are travelling on, that people of the previous generations haven't gone through. Many people experience the same situation as you do, and there are many people in the world whose situation is more terrible than yours. You name it—loss of job,

---
[45] https://en.wikipedia.org/wiki/Hans_Langsdorff

divorce, death, bankruptcy, debt, terminal illness, failure, abandonment, rejection, infertility, injustice, blackmail, discrimination, abuse, harassment, broken relationship, war, famine, natural disasters, and so on. People in difference part of the world are going through similar agonizing pain.

*Lying thought #4*: "I have no one to share my feeling with." This is absolutely untrue; there are lots of people and groups you can share your problems and challenges with. Thinking you are alone can cause a little smoke to turn into a fire, consuming the fabric of your soul. It is untrue to think that you have nobody to give anxiety and depression the ground in which to grow deep spreading roots. There are people around you with whom you can share your problems. Why don't you consider people like your parents, partner, siblings, teachers, pastors, humanitarian organization, healthcare professionals, counsellors, government established agencies, and ultimately God through prayers? The help and support you need is always around, if you are willing to look for it.

*Lying thought #5*: "Nobody will believe me." This is not true. People who care about you and your well-being will listen to you. They will support you because they believe in you. They know we are human and that we all have issues in our life. They will believe, because they have their own problems. There is no super-human anywhere, and no one can claim that everything about them is perfect. We have strengths as well as weaknesses. Our weaknesses may cause us to fail, but we must bounce back in hope, believing that we can be successful. When we lack motivation, when the burden of life is too heavy for us to bear, and when our mind is in confusion, we can find hope, peace, and joy when we share our burden. You can always find people who will believe your story and provide you with information that will offer the solution to your problems. Even if you are skeptical of finding a compassionate heart and attentive ear to hear you out, just pray and ask for God's help.

*Lying thought #6*: "I need to be alone to feel better." This is a big lie. The truth is that loneliness kills faster than many illnesses in our world today. When people isolate themselves from other people, they open the door wide for depression and suicidal thoughts. Loneliness is not a friend and should not be let in by anyone who desires a great life. The greatest weapon of emotional trouble is isolation. As soon as it hits someone, it tries to take the victim into captivity to enslave them. It will continuously bombard them with the thought that the more they stay away from people, the better they will feel. Socializing and exercise are tools to ease stress. When you belong to a group, attend meetings, and exercise more often, you empower both your physical heart and intellectual body to build resilience. You need friends, and your friends need you.

# Chapter Ten:
## Overcoming Self-complexes

Self is a person's essential being that distinguishes them from others. It is also an individual's awareness of his or her essential nature. It is considered as the object of someone's own thoughts, feelings, and sensations.

Human beings are complex. We are rational beings, and our behaviours are not mechanical. The complexity of human nature accounts for why people are unpredictable. Our temperament and character are unique, so are our values and desires which are manifested in who we show ourselves to be. There are two main categories of our self-complex: superiority and inferiority.

The way you see yourself can affect how you carry yourself. You will exude either confidence or fear, and your self-complex will impact how you relate to people and how successful you are in achieving your dream. There can be extremes in the concept of self. A superiority complex exists on the extreme high end of the scale, whereas an inferiority complex is situated on the extreme low end. Superiority is projected towards the high end and towards the low end lies the inferiority/moderate perception of self.

The information presented here will help readers examine themselves to discover where they belong on the self-complex scale, and to begin the process of self-transformation where it is necessary. It is high time for you to develop confidence, improve self-image, and ultimately become who you are created to be. Let's explore the domain of self and its compositions.

## Superiority Complexes
*Self-sufficiency*
Self-sufficiency is the condition of thinking or practice in which one manifests an egoistic nature and prides oneself on the ability to provide for oneself. It is being contented to a fault, self- satisfied, and unconcerned about others. This is especially true when pride and arrogance are influencing factors. Self-sufficiency is also the condition of being contentedly confident of one's ability.

When self-sufficiency develops into complacency, it becomes a problem. It gives an individual a superiority mentality in his dealings to the point that he no longer see obvious flaws in his life. The person becomes someone with dominant behaviour patterns who does things in a way to show off. A person with a self-sufficiency complex takes matters into his/her own hands and has no regards for other people.
Self-sufficiency places people in a position where they think they are too important, all knowing, powerful, and skillful to ask for help. They treat and manage other people without respect and never recognize the possibility of help from a greater being.

Self-sufficient people love to be in control and never want to be controlled. When you give them an opportunity to lead, they will discharge their duties with dominating confidence and authority. They think they can make it alone and love to command and manipulate people to gain their respect.

Most people with a self-sufficiency complex are extroverts, whose temperaments are characterized by a strong-will, a domineering spirit, and an authoritative nature. They think highly of themselves and do not care about other people's opinions, knowledge, or skills. They think that they know it all and can better accomplish a task alone rather than as a team. The few introverts that belong to this category tend to be perfectionists, as is the nature of melancholies.

*Self-approval*
Self-approval is a condition or episode of judging oneself to be right, and thinking and speaking favourably of oneself. It is the lifestyle and character of feeling, showing, and expressing oneself in a manner to gain a favourable opinion or commendation. It also connotes the state of being overly concerned about one's appearance and judgements other people makes about you.

In order to discover individuals with self-approval complex, examine their motives and goals. When they offer help generously to people in need, or show kindness, they do so with the goal of gaining attention and popularity. They always want people to notice them and praise them for what they are doing. All of their efforts and struggles in life are to achieve the goal of being noticed and have "worshippers." However, this type of lifestyle can undermine our ability to learn and grow. It can prevent us from taking responsibility when we make mistakes. It can destroy who we are, because when evaluate ourselves by what people say, we open ourselves to confusion and instability.

If you think you may have a self-approval complex, consider the following questions. Do you always expect thanks for everything you do for people? When you don't get their praise, do you withhold help from them? Do the words and actions of other people compel you to measure up to them— especially in terms of spending and purchasing? Are you easily irritated when other people talk about themselves? Do you frown at skillful individuals who seem to be better than you? Do you feel disappointed when your friends, colleagues, or family members do not comment on your effort at work, your appearance, or your opinion?

The frustration that people with self-approval complexes feel often shows up when their efforts to get people's attention, admiration, and appreciation aren't working. Their feelings and thinking are followed by regret and bitterness. Next, their behaviour will change; they will stop being the nice, because they were not appreciated. This could develop into further grievances or feelings of jealousy and stinginess. This can become dangerous, because these individuals think they are being deprived of reward for being nice. They want recognition as though their life depended on it.

If you are the person described above, you can transform your life by making the decision to be yourself. Being yourself requires knowing that you are different and unique, and that you are not under obligation to impress people or live up to their standards. Do things that make you happy and fulfilled. Live a normal life rather than a life that hinges on people's opinion.

*Self-opinion*
Individuals who form self-opinion about themselves are those people, who have excessive, immoderate, and inappropriately high opinions of themselves. They are the individuals who think themselves as flawless, both in speech and in what they do. They think they are perfect and are not willing to change such thoughts and feelings. These individuals have a high opinion of themselves and find it difficult to accept or approve of other people's feelings, or thoughts, about any subject matter.

Self-opinionated people are self-absorbed. They retain their opinion about themselves without a thorough reflection. When they think that something is right, they will refuse or be reluctant to give it careful and long consideration, and they will refuse to accept and consider another point of view.

Self-opinionated people are defensive. They are always prepared to stand against any expression of thought or suggestion that seems to attack or undermine their opinion of themselves. They reject constructive criticism and always cover up their failures with excuses and by blaming others. These individuals don't like to take responsibility for their mistakes or failures. They avoid people whose opinion they can't undermine—people whose ideas are superior and more powerful than theirs. This is because they always want to protect their pride.

Self-opinionated people are offensive and can show aggression when their opinions are not welcomed. In a meeting where everyone can make a suggestion or contribute, they don't want anyone to say anything that will contradict their opinion. They always like their opinion to be the last and best. When someone speaks after they have spoken, they see it as an attempt to put down their suggestions. These individuals can be insulting, rude, abusive, and quarrelsome when trying to compel everyone else to accept their thoughts and feelings about a subject. They indulge in unnecessary arguments and disagreeing with other suggestions.

Self-opinionated people are also authoritative. They always want to be in command of people and things. They have a domineering attitude and act in a manner that is harsh and humiliating. They give their opinion, even when nobody wants it. And when they do so, they often back it up with persuasive words or actions that can push other people into accepting or implementing their ideas.

You must start by being less generous with your opinions to help yourself out of this. Stop giving your opinion when nobody wants it. Another thing you should do is to start cultivating the attitude of acceptance. In order to do so, start listening to other people's thoughts and feelings, start considering their views, and show approval of good suggestions, even when they do not come from you. Accept this truth and the reality that your opinion and perception about things can be imperfect.

There will be times when other people's suggestions, based on their knowledge and experiences, can be better than yours. When you start accepting this fact, you will start welcoming and trying out other people's opinions. This will help you develop a teamwork spirit. It will also make it easier for people to approach you with their own ideas to help you in the times of your difficulties. In addition, it will make it easier for people to constructively commend or criticize you, which in the end will produce great success in your life and with other people.
Self-comparison

Self-comparing individuals are measuring themselves—their worth, qualifications, results, successes, achievements, etc.—against other people. They have a mental scale with which they weigh their own respect and praise and compare it to that of their friends, colleagues, partners, or neighbours. Self-comparing individuals often rank themselves higher than other people.

The fundamental problems experienced by self-comparing individuals are jealousy and envy. They develop envy and jealousy when they consider themselves to have less worth and value in comparison to other people. When they discover that someone whom they have rated below their standard is better off or more successful than they are, they develop the spirit of criticism and hatred toward them. They rarely celebrate other people's success and often develop false pride and treat people with disregard.
People of this sort fail to understand and accept that anybody can be

above them in everything. There will always and continuously be someone who, somehow and in some way, is better than them. You may be better in sports, while someone else is a better writer. You will never be the only person who can be above all other persons.

Self-comparison is dangerous; it destroys relationships. This is because people who compare themselves with other people often disregard other people's gifts and talents. They do not pay attention to what other people are doing, because in their minds they think they know better and can do better than others. This can breed anger and resentment in their heart toward people whom they believe are inferior.

To save yourself from this menace, you've got to stop comparing with others. Concentrate on developing and improving yourself, replace your self- comparison mentality with self-discovery and the development of positive feelings and thoughts. Appreciate the uniqueness and creative nature in other people, and in return other people will appreciate you.

*Self-confidence*
Self-confidence is a mental and emotional state in which individuals feel positive or convinced in their ability to do the things, they have set their mind to do. Self-confident people do not give any room to doubt or fear. They carry the motivation and enthusiasm that keeps them on track and undistracted. They continuously picture and feel the end they desire as though they are already there, which in turn gives them the assurance that they will meet their goal.

People often think that self-confident people are over-assured, which is not always the truth. Although there exists a fine line between over-confidence and healthy confidence, one should not mistake one for the other. It is wrong to assume that someone who has promised himself to stay on a course, no matter the challenge is over-confident. Unlike confident people, over-confident people do not acknowledge or accept the fact that their efforts toward their goals may not result in desired success. People who have healthy confidence do not always think that they are absolutely in control of everything, even when there are obvious faults and identifiable flaws that could mar their anticipated rewards. Excessive self-confidence hinders opportunity for improvement and change.

Knowledge and experience are the keys to heightening anyone's confidence. This involves continuous learning and practicing. That is how skills are developed and confidence is built. People who have the skill and knowledge to do certain tasks well, because they have practiced them, are usually confident of themselves. They are highly motivated and focused individuals who have a positive attitude in whatever they do.

The key to self-confidence is certainty, and the keys to certainty are belief in one's abilities and freedom from fear and doubt. It is normal to have some doubt, but if you practice and gain relevant experience in what you are set to do, it becomes easier to be free from fear of failure and doubt of your capacity to succeed.

### *Inferiority and Moderate Complexes*
Inferiority complex is an unrealistic feeling of general inadequacy. It is the doubt and unbelief in one's capacity to perform. It is caused by actual or supposed mental perception of uncertainty in one sphere, sometimes marked by moderate or aggressive behaviour in compensation.

When people feel inferior or have a moderate complex, their ability to express themselves is impaired; they can become nervous and bury their head in shame while there is actually no reason to do so. Inferiority complex affects individuals who have not come to the full knowledge of their abilities. There is always a time in life when one has to stand to prove themselves in the face of new challenges. There will always come a time to use creativity and critical thinking to solve problem. People with inferiority complexes can easily be drown in the ocean of new challenges—not because they lack the capability to turn things around, but because they can't trust what they have not proven.

The following description elucidates various types of inferiority and moderate complex (starting with moderate complex), and how people with demoralizing and demeaning self-complexes can transform their thinking and in a careful, deliberate manner transform their lives.

*Self-interest*
Self-interested people are those who are always concerned with or pay attention to themselves—those who care only for the things that appeal to their own feelings and thoughts. Self-interested people accept only the things or people who in their mind deserve their attention. They are often influenced by personal and selfish motives. They consider and approve things and other people based on their own self interests.

Self-interested individuals fall under moderate inferiority complex. The self-essentials of self-interested individuals can share attributes from both sides—superiority and inferiority complexes. The attributes of self-interested individuals are more of an introvert nature than an extrovert one. I made the choice to categorize them under inferiority complexes. Self-interested people share few attributes with self-opinionated individuals, but many attributes with individuals with inferiority complexes. They are predominately introverts. Self-interested people are self-absorbed. When they show that they care, they do so mainly to those whom they think they like most. They rarely care about people they don't know, and rarely help a stranger who is in desperate need of their help.

They are often the most confused individuals when it comes to decision- making—in their career, business, or relationships. This sometimes makes it difficult for them to be decisive in choosing career or business paths, as they always depend on their feelings more than their reasoning and natural talents. They sometimes delay in making decisions because they are still waiting for their feelings—even when immediate action is required.

Self-interested people are opportunity misers and wasters—they seldom stay on a course to the end because they often lose interest in it. They rarely take up an opportunity, no matter how profitable and important it might be for them, if it does not appeal to their feelings. They can jump from one career to another in a continuous search for the one that will most appeal to their feelings.

Self-interested people do not always take all the steps that are required in a task—especially when they do not like the people, they are going to do it with. It is natural to not always like every person and the way they do things, but self-interested people always want everything to revolve around them. They want all things to be expressed with "I" rather than "we," "you," or "they."

Individuals with self-interest can balance their life by learning to listen and accept constructive criticism. They grow their people skills through participation and working with other people's ideas and suggestion. They have to discipline their own impulses and choose to dive into opportunities that come their way with the determination to remain committed till the end.

*Self-rejection*

Self-rejection is the condition in which one refuses to accept, acknowledge, or believe in oneself or one's capacity to achieve a goal. Self-rejection results from the belief that there is a deficiency in one's life. This "deficiency" may be real or imaginary. It could be that an individual's opinion of someone is not correct, or that someone has the wrong opinion of themselves.

There are many reasons why individuals see deficiencies in themselves. These supposed deficiencies include, but are not limited to, physical appearance, parental background, educational background, race, poverty or penury, lack of eloquence, and failures in career, business, or relationships. Devastating experiences like rape, child abuse, betrayal, accusations, and mockery can produce a self-rejecting nature in someone; however, the main reasons for self-rejection are fear and doubt.

Unlike self-sufficient people, self-rejecting people see themselves as incapacitated in almost everything. They are afraid of failure, and as a result they do not act due to the fear of doing something incorrectly. They have the mentality and attitude of "I can't" or "I won't be able." As a result, they are reluctant to do things that they really could do with a snap of their fingers. They often procrastinate until someone shows up and gets it done. They lack enthusiasm and the motivation to develop their skills to advance their lives. They live in constant fear, even though they may wish to be free and force their way out of their cycle of self-rejection.

The root causes of self-rejection are ignorance and fear. Ignorance is the condition of being unaware, uninformed, or absence or lack of knowledge. It is the foundation of fear. Ignorance makes you believe you cannot do something that you would naturally do. Fear makes you believe you cannot do what you have been trained to do, and it can make you fall behind others who have had the same training as you. It can even make you dread doing things for which you have been commended in the past.

To determine if you have self-rejection or struggling with it, ask yourself the following questions. What if I do or say something wrong? What if I show up late at work? What if I fail to finish my task at the stipulated time? What if I make some mistakes? What if my supervisor or boss comes around and finds me doing something wrong? What if I'm misunderstood? The list goes on and on.

In order to gain freedom from self-rejection, you need to acknowledge it. You need to master the emotions of fear and anxiety and embrace confidence. You must develop the attitude of assurance and reassurance by learning and practice. You must believe and trust your ability to accomplish a task effectively and efficiently. It begins in the mind. It is a matter of choice. You can start thinking "I can do it." It's all about you and your decisions.

*Self-pity*
Self-pitying people have exaggerated self-indulgent attitudes and do things to attract sympathy from other people. They do this to make people see their unfortunate experiences so that they will help or show them mercy.

Self-pity is the opinion one has of oneself that makes one feel poor, deprived, or disadvantaged. Although unpleasant situations and unfair treatment can lead to short periods of self-pity, you should not allow this feeling to take root in your life. Don't start telling people things like, "He is treating me in this way because I am not as educated as he is " or "I know I will fail and not amount to anything in life."

Self-pity is like a prison to the human soul. It brings its victim under bondage. Its prisoners are always preoccupied and dominated with the feeling of their own difficulties, hardship, and sufferings to the point that they will disregard any possible way to build hope and strength to overcome their situations. It surrounds its prisoners with fear, doubt, suspicion, and low self-esteem.

Freedom from self-pity comes through the knowledge that pity is a pit that holds its captive down and never wants to let go. Make the move forward towards your goal while staying focused on it. Push yourself out, seek to perform and outperform yourself among people around you. Work hard on your financial freedom. Deal with issues that make you grieve, and resolve matters in a manner that settles an issue convincingly or produces a definite result.

*Seeing Yourself the Right Way*
Your self-opinion is the view others have of you that you have accepted to be the true description of who you are. People's opinions about you are usually based on their personal perception of your character or the personality you display. It also refers to how you see yourself.
We go through life with lots of labels and descriptions. We carry the opinions or perceptions we have about ourselves that come from what we think of ourselves or from what other people think about us. Often, we are faced with the choice of either accepting who we believe we are or what other people tell us we are. When we choose to believe other people's opinions about ourselves, we tend to either push ahead and do certain things to prove them right, or seek to be the opposite of what others think of us.

The right way of seeing yourself is all about understanding who you are and what you are made up of. It is in understanding your strengths and mastering your weaknesses. It is positioning yourself both physically and mentally to acquire all it takes to advance your career and destiny. It is exerting pressure or making a great effort to lift yourself from where you are to where you ought to be. It is not a matter of self-sufficiency, self-approval, self-interest, self-opinion, self-comparison, or self-pity; it's the discovery of the unique attributes you possess. You can then transform your weaknesses into useful virtues to benefit yourself and others.

The two fundamental factors that can help you achieve any change you desire in life are your mentality and your functionality. Your mentality comprises how much you know and how much you are willing to learn, which then determines what you think and how you view yourself. Your thought patterns and the internal descriptions shape your life. If you constantly think about failure, you will never win. But if you think constantly about success, you will often win.

Your functionality is the second factor that can shape your life. While in school, we learned a very important truth about genetics, and I later discovered a saying in the scriptures that support it. In genetics, I learned a theory of Lamarck. Jean-Baptiste Pierre Antoine de Monet, Chevalier de Lamarck (1 August 1744–18 December 1829), often known simply as Lamarck, was a French naturalist and a soldier, biologist, academic, and early proponent of the idea that biological evolution occurred and proceeded in accordance with natural laws. He gave the term "biology" a broader meaning by coining the term for special sciences, chemistry, meteorology, geology, and botany-zoology.[46] The theory is often referred to as the Law of Use and Disuse. It states that: The parts of an organism's body that are used become more developed; parts that are not used become smaller and may disappear. When you don't use a feature that you have, it becomes distinct.

When you don't make the effort to discover what you possess so you can put it to use, or you don't put to use that which you know you

---
[46] https://en.wikipedia.org/wiki/Jean-Baptiste_Lamarck

have, it will gradually disappear regardless of its value or importance. Practitioners are people who put their gifts, talents, knowledge, and skills to work. However, if practitioners don't practice, they become outdated in their field of study.

Another factor that can transform your life is being positive about your life and destiny. If you believe it, say it. Your tongue is a powerful tool for creating that which you desire. As you move toward achieving a goal, speak of how successful you will be. It works miracles. It drives away fear and invites confidence. Never base your opinion about yourself on what other people say about you. While they sometimes can confirm what you know and think about yourself, be careful to know the difference. If you always base your opinion about yourself on what other people say, you can lose your focus and sense of direction. For example, if you only hang around with flatterers, they could open you up to developing selfish syndromes—self approval, self-opinion, self-comparison, and so on.

The right way of seeing yourself entails being rational and honest about your lifestyle and judgement. It requires you to accept criticism where and when necessary. Some criticism can be far more important than praise. It can reveal your flaws so you can consciously adjust your approach and strategy to remain on track. It also can help you change your approach of pursuing your goal to get there faster. It is important to note that not all criticism is rewarding; bowing to all criticism can make you confused. Some criticism can hinder growth and can ruin one's destiny. That is why; put the acquisition of wisdom first in all that you strive to acquire in life. Wisdom puts you in charge of your life and destiny. It helps you know right from wrong, and the fear of God is the beginning of wisdom.

The ability to handle discouragement and criticism wisely is strategic in bringing out the best in you. When you listen to constructive criticism and properly rationalize it in a manner that will bring a positive impact to your life, you'll start having a balanced life. But if you only listen to those who tell you what a great person you are, you will soon fall. If your critics' opinions define who you are, and you take them without rationalizing such views with great wisdom, you will be locked in a circle of criticism from which you will never rise.

In your effort to discover your special gifts and potential and put them to work, watch out for the enemy called pride. Pride is a destroyer. It results from pleasure or satisfaction taken in an achievement, possession, or association. When you listen to the music of your praises, and it gets into your head, you are not far from pride.

You can be in control of situations if you are having a balanced lifestyle. It is a fact that you cannot please everybody all the time. It is a waste of time and effort to try to impress all people because some may never be completely impressed. On the other hand, stop living in isolation (avoiding people), it will block your opportunity for self-discovery and improvement. There is every need to know how to interact with people or work with individuals of different mentalities and personalities. There are many things to learn in association, and there are bridges to cross as well. However, you must see yourself from the right perspective. It doesn't matter what others say. Remember you are unique and to attain the peak of your destiny, you must live an original life.

*Building Your Self-Esteem and Improving Your Self-Worth*
Every individual is wired with the capacity to do great things, achieve great results, and have resounding success. So why do many fail and only a few succeed? My answer is that people fail for two reasons—either they think they can't succeed (and block necessary information that will help them to succeed), or they have never tried—or tried and gave up (too soon) on their way to success. Other reasons could

include past failures and setbacks. These are the reasons why those who tried and failed are not willing to try again and again.

Positive self-image and confidence are vital to success. These are the reasons behind all great accomplishments, whether big or small. You can rise to the top irrespective of all the things you consider as weaknesses because you possess intangible strengths that when released can produce in you and for you the very result you desire. Here is an example:

A company that sold encyclopedias door to door hired a new guy without interviewing him. Later, he was trained through correspondence. Thereafter, he started selling encyclopedias. Three months later, the company's manager tells the president, "Boss, the guy we trained through mail has just broken our sales record."
"I want to find out how he did it," the president orders.

A week later ... "Boss, I met the guy. He has a stuttering problem," remarked the manager.
"How can he sell?" asked the president.
"He knocks on doors and when people open he asks, 'would you like to bu... bu... bu... bu... but... an encyclo... cyclo... cyclo...pedia? Or would you ra... ra... ra... ra... ra... ra... rather... I... I... re... re... read it... to you?' So they buy!"

What do you think about the guy in the above story? Whatever your answer, you probably won't believe that this guy believed in himself. He had conquered the discouraging opinion that because he stammers, he can't be a good marketer. That's what I expect from you after reading this book. I expect you to have a good self-image and self-esteem that will help you see beyond every limitation you can think of or imagine.

Self-esteem is both a mental and emotional state in which someone has values that exalt, improve, encourage, motivate, or project them in their personal views about themselves. It springs from a belief system, core values, and an admiration of one's inward knowledge, strength, and attitude that enables them to fully express their strength for maximum impact or result. It includes the attitude one shows inwardly when no one else is watching and outwardly when other people are watching.

To improve your self-worth and build your self-esteem, you must first be mindful and watch what you think or hear. What you hear can have a way of getting into what you think about, and what you think about obviously determines who you become. Mind what you think and meditate on, because negative thought produces negative energy, but positive thought produces positive outcomes. Giving in to negative thoughts will discourage and degrade you internally and externally. Do not allow discouraging thoughts to dominate your thinking. Choose to hear inwardly and outwardly words that produce confidence and faith. Never underestimate yourself.

Secondly, to improve your self-worth, you must detach yourself from negative people, environments, and materials. Surround yourself with positive people. I do not mean your trumpeters or those who sing your praises. I mean those who will agree with you when you are right and tell you in your face when you do wrong things. As for the environment, do not stay around places where bad things are promoted. Do not dwell on negative situations. Don't bring past troubles into the present.

Last but not least, you must strive to continuously improve yourself, or else you will become outdated and lose your value. Be broad in learning. Improve both your general and specialized knowledge. Always update to the latest knowledge available. You will gain more confidence through unreserved learning and training. Knowledge boosts your intellect as well as your self-assurance. Think about this statement: The difference between the successful and the unsuccessful is that the successful are acting on what they know, while the unsuccessful do not know or are not doing. Be versatile in learning. Learn for these two reasons: (1) To help yourself and (2) To help others.

ELISHA O. OGBONNA

# Chapter Eleven:
## Guide for Handling Problem Emotions

*Understanding How Feelings Work*
The understanding of emotions begins with the understanding that feelings are neither right nor wrong. If you have certain feelings, whether negative or positive, those feelings do not make you good or bad. Feelings come naturally, although events can also trigger them. They are stirred up when something happens or when we are afraid that something bad will happen.

Don't believe it when you hear the words, "You should feel that way" or "You shouldn't be emotional about the loss of your dear one" or "You shouldn't be angry when you are hurt." Those are the words that friends, colleagues, or well-wishers use to try to cheer you up when bad things happen to you. But contrary to their expectations, these words do not actually make anyone who is in pain or sorrow feel better. Rather, these can make you feel worse.

What should one do when experiencing a variety of emotions, especially troubling, devastating, or discouraging ones?

When you experience hurt or emotional pain that threaten your life—do not repress (hide or deny) such feeling(s). Do not condemn yourself when you have negative feelings. Events make some feelings come naturally, and when that happens, do not pretend you do not have them. For example, if someone bumps into you and walks away without saying a word, it can make you feel angry. You didn't get angry for no reason. Someone did something to you and did not acknowledge it was wrong and their fault. When things of this kind happen, hiding or denying such feelings hinders healing and amplifies hurt.

When you acknowledge that the person who has bumped into you has hurt your feelings, you have at least identified the root cause of your feeling of hurt. When you fail to acknowledge this hurt, you unconsciously store it in your inner world (heart). As time goes on, and different people at different times hurt you, these hurts will pile up and become mixed up such that you may not be able to separate each feeling and what caused it. At this point, it will start affecting how you make sense of your life—often in a negative way. You may start thinking that you are not likeable or cannot be a member of a team. These negative interpretations of yourself will make you susceptible to depression, anxiety, malice, and all sorts of troubling emotions that can gain root into your personality and change your lifestyle.

Another part of understanding how feelings work is recognizing that your feelings do not dictate your options or invalidate your choices. You may have a bad experience that produces bad feelings in you, but you can choose not to respond to the bad experience with bad actions. You can make good choices about how you want to handle the situation. To make the right decisions about your feelings, you must understand the root causes of the feelings and process their effects on you in a healthy way.

*Processing Feelings in Healthy Ways*
Our thinking and knowledge about feelings is fundamental to how we respond to unfavourable, devastating, or uncomfortable life

experiences. They are part of the most determinant factors in our attitude and personalities. How we think of and interpret a situation in our mind determines the choice we will make in responding to that situation. When we broaden our knowledge in the area of emotions, it empowers and directs us when deciding on the best approach for dealing with threatening experiences. By asking the question, "Why do I feel the way I feel about this situation?" you open up both your conscious and unconscious mind to drawing insight from the wealth of knowledge you have banked within you. However, when you ask, "Why is he treating me this way?" you place yourself in-between two courses—either judging the offender and his actions or judging yourself for being found in the situation.

When you take the path of judging the offender, you will analyze him to figure out if what he did was intentional or not. If you think it is intentional, you start analyzing the gravity of his "wicked" heart and personality. If you think it was not intentional, you will be compelled to review your part in the event. Your past experiences merge with the current one and become more intense so that if you are not careful, you can develop hatred and malice, which can further lead to revenge.

Since no one can be totally free from offense as long as we live on this planet and interact with other people, we need to discover how best to process our feelings, especially threatening feelings and the feelings of hurt. When you accept this truth, you will begin to align your thoughts and attitude toward finding the best way to respond to your experiences.

When you harbour evil in your heart and brood over it, it will cause you to react negatively to what has happened to you. It is to understand that you are not dragged into trouble by what happens to you but by how you react to what happens to you. It is not the temptation to sin that makes people sinners but rather the yielding to the temptation. It is not wholly the temptation that produces your action but rather the decision from your analysis and understanding of the situation. When feelings are not processed in a healthy way, the resultant effect may bring trouble.

Do you know the difference between thoughts of harm and harmful thoughts? The difference between the two lies between the analysis of an event and the paralysis that may go alongside it. While thoughts of harm come from what has happen and enter our mind uninvited, they become harmful thoughts only when we allow them to impair our interpretation and cause us to harm someone.

In order to process feelings in a healthy way, it includes knowing the appropriate time and way to express our feelings. This is because there are times when it is important to hold on (especially in the heat of the moment when you and the other person are both furious) and express feelings later. There are also times when you should express your feelings right away, but it has to be done with the right approach and proper use of words.

Always remember that how you process your feelings about an event in your mind determines how you will express your feelings. The more you allow feelings of hurt or pain to linger in your heart, the more you endanger your life and become subject to bitterness, malice, hatred, revenge, or depression. When you choose to delay an action that might be harmful, it allows you to think further and make a better decision. To do this, you need to employ your reasoning power to distinguish and clarify feelings emanating from the experience.

Before you act, you must complete this process and adjust yourself to it. You need lots of knowledge of people and why they do certain things in a certain way. Thorough knowledge of various kinds of temperaments is recommended because it will help you to understand human character and make decisions on how to relate to people. You need to know your limits and that although you cannot change people, you can consciously—with the right approach—influence their attitude toward you.

One more thing to note is that when there is conflict between the mind and the emotions (especially when your mind is less empowered by positive knowledge and insight), the emotions always win. And if emotions are not properly harnessed, they could endanger one's life. What you think affects the way you feel, and the way you feel affects the way you think. For example, you would interpret a little child hitting you differently than an adult hitting you. Your interpretation of each of these events will be different. When your emotions are high, give them a rest, but do not deny or suppress them. Engage your reasoning ability along with your intention to make peace and not war; you will see that the situation will turn out better.

*Expressing Feelings in Healthy Ways*
Compulsive individuals often argue that some inner force compels them to do things the wrong way, but what they do in reality is what they choose to do—even if it doesn't feel like a choice. This statement might be very challenging and unacceptable to such people, but it is true. We have the ability to choose our responses to our experiences in life that's how we are created. When we are confronted by a number of options, we decide which one is most satisfactory to us.

The vital key to commanding our emotions is to express our feelings in a healthy way. The argument over who's right or wrong will not solve a problem, but instead worsen a situation. I once read a story about a man who was taken to court because he had punched a neighbour in the nose. The man claimed in his defense that he had to do what he did because his neighbour had insulted his wife. The court verdict was this: "No, you chose to do it. Pay the fine."

We engage willpower to express our feeling. The will is the faculty of choosing or choice-making. It is the factor of expression. Our personality is usually described by our expressions or manner of expressions. Humans do not operate in isolation. One usually aligns oneself to cooperate and follow the direction in which the mind and emotion is leading.

When you reason with your mind about an ugly experience you had and dwell on it for a long time, your interpretation can be heightened as your imagination gets involved. Once your imagination is involved, it becomes difficult to deal with the situation all by yourself. You may need to seek advice from someone who knows better, or pray to God for help. This is because human imagination is more powerful than human will.

For example, when you set your mind (with your imagination involved) in one direction and your will in another direction, your imagination ultimately will win. This may lead to negative actions if your mind (and imagination) is determined to return hurt for hurt while your will wants to forgive your offender. Many people who are not aware of this get themselves into trouble and give into negative thoughts. Then they wonder why they have done that which they "chose" not to do.

Many people say, "But I thought I had a strong will. I am a principled person. What happened?" Others have said, "I quit this or that habit," but then they get back into the same thing. Flabbergasted, they ask, "What happened?" They have fallen prey to temptation. The answer is clear and precise. It was because their will (decision) conflicted with their imagination (or mind), and the will lost to the mind.

Therefore, it is not advisable and feasible to attempt to develop a strong will without bringing your imagination into agreement with your will. The important part of mastering your emotions is finding a way to direct or redirect your thinking (imagination). And if there is a conflict between the two, the imagination will win every time.

You must always feed your mind with positive and inspiring virtues to charge of it. Remember the joy of doing good deeds and then draw on this when you need to be encouraged and motivated to live a life full of love. You will teach your mind to love, give, and forgive without struggle—the three ingredients that makes relationships healthy and successful.

*Practice and Make Forgiveness a Lifestyle*
Forgiveness is the act of excusing a mistake, hurt, or offense by refraining from imposing punishment on an offender or demanding satisfaction for an offense. It is the act of renouncing anger or resentment against someone who has hurt you by letting the hurt pass by. It is granting pardon without harbouring resentment. Forgiveness is a personal act; no one can order you to forgive. It is by choice. You can choose either to forgive or hold onto resentment.

Those who practice and make forgiveness a lifestyle habitually performs the act of letting go of an offense. They surrender their right to get even and the desire to return hurt for hurt. They refuse to hate the offender and no longer desire for the offender to suffer for what he has done. They know human nature is weak and imperfect and they may offend someone someday.

We can develop our capacity to forgive by making forgiveness a habit through constant practice and repeated performance. The gateway to freedom and advancement in life is by learning how to forgive and choosing to forgive our offenders. This is because it sets at liberty both the victim of the offense and the offender. It prevents future problems that the hurt can bring to both individuals. It washes away the stain of hurt and brings relief to the pains that it carries alongside.

You must understand what it means to be hurt and why hurt must not be allowed to stay in anyone's heart in order to develop the capacity to forgive. There are individual differences, and people see and do things differently. Everyone behaves and does things to the level of information and knowledge they have. When people do not understand the purpose of a thing, they are susceptible to abusing it. People can do what they do either deliberately or ignorantly. You cannot control people's thoughts and actions. Besides, you should understand that you have, or will someday, hurt someone's feelings yourself—whether consciously or unconsciously. You need to know that sometimes people do things that hurt others' feelings without the slightest knowledge of what they have done.

To begin the process of forgiveness, you must acknowledge the hurt and your contribution to the person's reason for hurting you. After acknowledging and admitting your hurt, you must process the hurt in a healthy way. Processing a hurt in a healthy way entails finding out if you were hurt as a result of something you did wrong. If it is a result of your wrong doing, you should apologize otherwise, let the other person know that he has hurt your feelings. Even when it is difficult for you to reach out to him, still forgive. Forgiveness must be immediate, because both you and your offender need it.

In any relationship with the opposite sex, such as marriage, you must understand that there exist differences and what happens when one forgives other. You must understand and accept the fact that men and women think differently. As a result, it affects their perception and attitude of forgiveness. It affects as well the way of expressing feelings of hurt. There may be lingering feelings and unstoppable misunderstandings, and without good knowledge and understanding this can lead to separation in relationships.

After a misunderstanding or series of misunderstandings in a relationship, both parties can agree to forgive and forget. The man can forget but may not forgive, whereas the woman can forgive but may not forget. This is because of the differences that naturally exist in the make-up of men and women's emotions. When a new incident happens, a woman might bring up the past and remind the man of previous hurts that he has forgotten but not forgiven. When these past hurts are revived and refreshed, they merge with the current hurt to form a synergy that hurts deeper and may result in a separation.

If those in marriages could recognize this fact, I believe it would make room for more tolerance, and possibly, forgiveness and reconciliation. They will be able to protect their marriages from breaking down. It will help both man and woman to make forgiveness a constant attitude instead of adding more hurt to current injuries. When we make a promise, we should always keep it. When we break our promises, it makes members of our family feel insecure and rebellious, and we lose their trust and respect.

When you promise to forgive and have forgiven, try to understand what happened, identify and admit your role in the process why you were hurt. If you do find out that you did something wrong, this will prompt you to change your attitude and prevent you from bringing up the past. On the other hand, if you find out that you did nothing wrong, instead of holding resentment, forgive generously. Talk to your partner politely about your feelings only at the right time. This will help you to reunite with him or her in a wonderful way. It will cause your love for him or her and his or her love for you to grow deeper. Venting anger does not work and will never work in relationships. It can never solve a misunderstanding by bringing up the past; rather, it aggravates the misunderstanding.

It is important to note that after forgiving, the feeling of hurt does not often disappear immediately. Some pains can take time to clear off. You must be patient until the pain has gradually and completely gone away. Be patient with the healing process.

Another point to explain here is that forgiveness precedes reconciliation, although not all forgiveness ends up in reconciliation. Reconciliation means repairing or reestablishing the cordial relationship between you and someone who has hurt you, or someone whom you have hurt. Forgiveness opens the door to reconciliation, but the process of reconciliation is not complete until the offender recognizes and admits that the hurt he/she has caused was his/her fault. It is important that you still forgive no matter what—for the sake of your health, life, and destiny, and to release your offender from the prison of hatred and animosity. In this way, you can advance in your career and life.

# Chapter Twelve:
## Anonymous Threats: Emotional Risk and Safe Haven

Why do companies have suggestion boxes in different location in their building? Why would they provide incentives for employees' suggestions or make room for anonymity?

When I was working for a company three years ago, it had severe issue in dealing with new hires, who were quitting their job unannounced and within weeks of hiring. Also, others who stayed in their position often lasted fewer than three years. The management struggled to find the missing pieces of the puzzle to solve this problem. Even the oral and friendly conversation with older employees could not provide any positive results.

What could be the problem? This company had been successful and established businesses and other companies around the world. They offered an attractive employees benefit package for new hires who complete their three months probationary period. This package includes: health benefits (dental, eyes, physiotherapy and percentage reimbursement for other government uncovered health issues), gym membership fees reimbursement, one-week paid vacation after one year which increases by the number of years worked for the company; retirement plan in which they match any amount you signed up for direct bank's deposit.

Obviously, it got to be something beyond, apart from excellent employee's benefits. And in an effort to find the missing piece of the puzzle, the management called for a meeting and told every worker that the boxes have been set up at different locations. They encourage every worker to write their suggestions and opinions they might have toward the growth of the company, health and safety of employees, and other matters that would help the management in employees' affairs. The meeting was concluded with emphasis that the workers can remain anonymous if anyone fear reprisal or wish to hide their identity.

When I thought of their action and why it would be welcomed by the employees, it reminds me the purpose of whistleblower protection act, S.20 — 101st Congress (1989-1990): The purpose of this Act is to strengthen and improve protection for the rights of Federal employees, to prevent reprisals, and to help eliminate wrongdoing within the Government.[47] This is similar to Ontario Securities Commission which states, "The OSC will make all reasonable efforts to protect the identities of whistleblowers. Under the Ontario Securities Act, the OSC may take enforcement action against employers who take reprisals against whistleblowers."[48]

Anonymous can be a useful tool for obtaining information that one would not ordinarily have. This information includes the disclosure of illegality, waste, and corruption. Harassment, violence, unsafe operation or use of equipment, endangering oneself or others are among information that every organization would want to be notified about, which some employees would avoid reporting if they cannot remain anonymous. However, the major step toward a more effective

---

[47] Whistleblower Protection Act of 1989; https://www.congress.gov/bill/101st-congress/senate-bill/20/text]

[48] Whistleblower Protections; https://www.osc.gov.on.ca/en/protections.htm#:~:text=The%20OSC%20will%20make%20all,are%20represented%20by%20a%20lawyer

and efficient operations of any business depends partly on this information for training and improvement. It is also critical to help in eliminating wrongdoing within the system.

However, besides whistleblowing, research, questionnaires, survey, opinion, report or suggestions anonymity, like every other tool which can be used or abused. Anonymous can be used as a tool to intimidate, cause panic or hurt someone. When this is the case, anonymous is put into use as an instrument of threat or promised harm.

Anonymous threat can have significant and sometimes devastating impact in victim's life. Similarly, the comments, threat as well as antagonistic expression from social media trolls can wreck emotional havoc up to the point of depression and suicidal thoughts. Anonymous is a word that is used for a person who have unknown or unacknowledged name. People who choose to go anonymous do so to hide their identity and prevent their targets and victims from taking any action that would indict them. Troll is a social media slang for someone who starts posting insults, often laced with profanity or other offensive language on social media sites to intentionally upset their targets.

Unlike trolling, when messages or comments are sent to someone in an effort to do some harm, it is a threat. Threat is a statement of an intention to inflict pain, injury, damage, or other hostile action on someone in retribution for something done or not done. Social media perpetrators often hide under anonymity to shield themselves from being prosecuted. Social media threats, and letters of hate messages are recognized as criminal offence in many countries. This pushes back on unrestrained freedom of anonyms in expressing their grudges against the target individual.

Anonyms are generally those people, who do not welcome civil conversation and are not openly objectionable in their argument. They are individuals who attach importance to self-respect and as a result are self-opinionated. They will not move forward with an open mind or say openly how they feel about a situation. Although some anonyms may be people who know the target individual, however, in a greater sphere, these are people who are often inconsequential or of little importance to the target. People, who are disillusioned and have been severely disappointed up to the point of delusion are more likely to engage in anonymous threat. Also, people with undisciplined emotions could become enraged by their disappointing experiences, and instead of changing their approach would resort to finding someone to nail for their disappointing experiences. And in case if it happens to be someone they know, they may choose to go anonymous.

Some anonym may live in the same area as the targets and may have some way of witnessing the targets' emotional reactions to their attacks. Anonyms can be a family friend, a jealous employee, a neighbor, a family member or a political opponent sympathizer. Anonym persons may be people who has been indoctrinated, brainwashed or deceived into believing something that may not be true about their target. People, who have lost the ability to speak their mind in a civil manner or have been compelled to believe in propaganda and conspiracy theories, are more likely to repress their feeling and bury their opinion to anonymous threat. The rage, rashness, false accusation, threat or even projected physical violence can wreck huge mental, emotional and physical havoc to the target.

There are four major P's of pressure, assault and threat. When there is room for interaction and an interdependent operation that involves two or more people, when the parties do not agree on same terms or if one perceive and the other is lacking behind in their part, there would be likelihood of pressure or threat. The four P's of pressure are: people, problem, penny and politics. These are major source of misunderstanding in life, family or workplace. Workplace harassment beside sex, gender, race, and ethnicity discrimination can be deeply hurtful to the point that the victim may choose a dangerous path to express their hurts.

Workplace is a place where people of different sex, gender, race, ethnicity, religion, and political views meets to work. As a result, top companies and organization avoid associating or giving their opinions especially on the two most conflicting affiliations - religion and politics. Even though there might be some policy in place advising people to refrain from discussion on these, workers would voice their opinion on these without cautions. This open doors for harassment and sometimes violence.

Workplace violence or occupational violence refers to violence, usually in the form of physical abuse or threat that creates a risk to the health and safety of an employee or multiple employees. Occupational Health and Safety Act (OHSA) Definition s. in Ontario:[49] "Workplace violence" means, the exercise of physical force by a person against a worker, in a workplace, that causes or could cause physical injury to the worker; an attempt to exercise physical force against a worker, in a workplace, that could cause physical injury to the worker; a statement or behaviour that it is reasonable for a worker to interpret as a threat to exercise physical force against the worker that could cause physical injury to the worker.

There are five major types of Workplace Violence Incidents, which include: criminal intent, customer/client dispute, employees' feud,

---

[49] https://www.ontario.ca/document/workplace-violence-school-boards-guide-law/workplace-violence-under-occupational-health-and-safety-act

personal/domestic violence, ideological conflict/provocation. The concise definition of each type is given below.

Type One – Criminal Intent: This refers to violence, the perpetrator has no legitimate relationship to the business or its employees and is usually committing a crime in conjunction with the violence (robbery, shoplifting, trespassing).

Type Two – Customer/Client dispute: This refers to violence in which the perpetrator has legitimate relationship to the business or its employees, but has been disappointed by quality, price or speed (QPS) and as a result lost emotional control by choosing to vent their anger through verbal or physical attack in order to release their grievance.

Type Three – Employees' feud: This refers to violence in which a worker that experiences a real or imagined wrong or other cause for complaint, especially unfair treatment by employer or fellow workers, attacks a colleague, who they perceived as the person has initiated their workplace problems either through verbal or physical assault.

Type Four – Personal/Domestic Violence: This refers to violence in which a partner that experiences a real or imagined wrong or other cause for complaint, especially unfair treatment at home chooses to attack the offending partner at a workplace or parking lot of the workplace either through verbal or physical assault.

Type Five – Ideological Conflict/Provocation: This refers to violence in which the perpetrator who experiences a real or imagined wrong or other cause for complaint, especially unfair treatment in their ideological beliefs chooses to attack the offending person or at a workplace, parking lot of the workplace, social media, and even visiting their residence to vent their anger through verbal, physical assault or media propaganda. The ideological beliefs of authoritarianism and social dominance can find their root in religious or political influences. Political and religious related ideologies are associated with violent conflict among extremist of the ideology. Ideological groups often share ideological beliefs in a passionate way and engage members deep rooted philosophy for either individual or collective action. They can circulate information that can spur violent action, once their legitimate target of violence is named or identified.

Political ideology has not gained as much awareness in workplace violence as it has today. At the societal level, particular political ideological has been instrumental to media wars and propaganda but with the advent of Covid-19, it is not infiltrating workplace like a pandemic virus as jobs are being swept off people's feet like a carpet. Politics seek to acquire and retain power. Ideology is usually part of any power structure, be it politics or religion.

*Dealing with Anonymous Threats*
*Trainning:*
It is not uncommon to have issues when people are brought together under one umbrella—work, religion, politics or organization. The various issues that employers will have to grapple with when not addressed properly at the onset of the business or in the company's policy through awareness and training, are the above mentioned five major workplace harassment and violence. With rapid growth of political ideology that is infiltrating the work systems, I think employers, union of workers and every worker should start asking for a review of the workplace policy to including political influences. It is important to carve out training for workers and placing important responsibilities on them, report or seek legal help in the event of unbearable pressure, threat and assault. Employers should be made to provide strategies to protect their employees or face the weight of the law when they fail to abide the rule. For example: Ontario employers

are required by law to have certain workplace policies in place at work.

The policies that employers must have include the following:
  i. a Workplace Health and Safety Policy;
  ii. a Workplace Violence and Harassment Policy;
  iii. an Accessibility Policy; and
  iv. a Pay Equity Plan (employers with 10 or more employees).

Failure to have these policies in place is a violation of Ontario law and may result in the imposition of statutory fines and penalties.

*Mental and Emotional Assessment*
The routine activities should be carried out weekly, monthly or quarterly to addresses any pattern of offending and or patterns of social interaction at the workplace that involves harassment or threat. This assessment can be included in companies risk assessment process. Risk assessment is the combined effort towards identifying and analyzing potential events that may negatively impact individuals, assets, and/or the environment; and making judgments "on the tolerability of the risk based on the risk analysis" while considering all other influencing factors.

***Threat Response Strategy***
Threat Response Planning is a process of identifying what you will do in an event of workplace threat. There are two types of threat that results from ideological violence—identified and Anonymous. The main threat response strategies for identified threats are in the acronyms of R-E-A-C-H and for Anonymous threats are in the acronyms of R-E-C-O-R-D.

As ideological based threat is growing and becoming normal, there is a need to push back in order to reduce or possibly eliminate the opportunities for assault. If there is an unprotected target and there are sufficient self-satisfying rewards, a passionate offender may commit a crime. Here are my opinions on how to deal with either situation.

*Identified threats.*
R – Review: This is a formal assessment or examination of something with the possibility or intention of instituting change, if necessary. If it is at work, review what you often talk at workplace, who reacted negatively, and the comments made. Also, check out the possibility of the individual's friend sharing the incident with another friend who would want to carry the act on their behalf.

E – Enquire/Ask: This is a formal act of asking for information from someone, colleague or professional on policy implication and standpoint with respect to the situation. You should gather all the information by reaching out to people who have experienced the same and once you have enough information you can begin investigation or track the anonymous yourself.

A – Announce: This involves revealing the identity of the Anonymous to people in your close contact. If there is room to have uncomfortable conversation, you may do so, if this individual is someone that would welcome civil conversation, otherwise it might be necessary to make a public and typically formal declaration about threat to higher authority that would look into the matter and seek to resolve the situation. Since Anonyms often fear the disclosure of their identity, and when it becomes clear that you know their identity, they could either be compelled to make peace or hasten their planned action. They would like to act fast or get a partner to do the same as long as they can, and stop the action once they feel their identity can be revealed. Meanwhile, it is important for the victim to think about what action to take especially if the identified Anonymous is someone that could be dangerous.

C – Consult with a lawyer or seek counseling: Anonymous, who happens to be a family member may wish to turn himself in for reconciliation. However, a stranger who for political or religious reason threatens to hurt you may be difficult to convert. Extremist of political parties as well as religious organization are usually dogged and rugged individual whose opinions cannot be easily swayed either by facts or figures. These are people with closed mind that would not want to hear or consider their opponent opinion. That is why it is important to seek advise on how to handle such identified Anonymous, especially with the manner of safeguarding your evidence and avoiding confrontation or allegations that would put you on the wrong side of defamation and possible lawsuit.

H – Hanker, harness and Hoist: The emotional trauma and sometimes mixed feelings associated with threat and combination of fear/anger emotional state may produce indecision as one may confuse with need to act and, wait and watch event play out on their own. There is every need to muster courage and have a strong desire to do something about the situation. Victims must hanker for action that would expose, stop and bring justice to perpetrator. This is because certain people do not learn when they are left of the hook easily. These types of people often go further to do far more than what they were let go from. Harness your information following your decision to take action. Report and follow up until something is done to get the perpetrator assures your safety by committing to retracting the threat. The next step is to hoist yourself out of the hurt and ensuing emotional trauma. This can be achieved through self-awareness, self-assurance and self-advancement.

*Anonymous threats*
The acronyms for actions that victims could take in the case of anonymous threat is explained with the word – RECORD. There are things you can do even when the identity of the individual threatening

you is hidden from you. These actions can help you identify the individual or stop their plan to attack you. They are:

R – Record: This is a formal establishment of a thing or constituting a piece of evidence about the past, especially on account of an act or occurrence, kept in writing or some other permanent form.

E – Evaluate the seriousness: This is a formal act of considering threat in order to make a judgment and determine the significance, worth, or nature of its gravity. Generally, when people are angry, they can say things that they would regret saying, but in the case of anonymous threat it takes them a while to issue threat which make their words and intention a premeditated and well thought-out. Take every anonymous threat seriously considering the action, that is threatened.

C – Create awareness: This involves being conscious of any threat and taking a deliberate action of letting people around you have cognizant of events. It is incredibly important that someone close to you and someone you can trust should know about the threat so they can keep an eye on you and the things happening around you. In that way, they can keep check on you for changes and be conscious before you take a dangerous step. They also loom at for sign and figure out the perpetrators.

O – Observe the threat: Some threats, especially anonymous may come from people around the victim. However, ideological inspired threat can come from any group of people that may be organized or unorganized. Observing the threat, recording and making notes could give clue to who the anonymous are and possibly who they are working for.

R – Report to the Authority: Reporting the threat to police is one of the smartest things to do because they can start their investigation early and track down the perpetrators before complete mayhem breaks out. Facebook, Instagram, Twitter etc. will unlikely provide the names of the anonymous attacker but can block or close their accounts. However, they are unlikely going to stop the police from getting the names of the individuals through court order or other means.

D – Deal with the emotional impact. This could be the grief of loss or the fear of the unknown. Process your experience in a healthy way by acknowledging your feelings, understanding that other people are also going through the same e.g., police, law makers, judges, political office holders and so on. Talk to someone or join a community that would provide you with support and encouragement which will speed up your healing and recovery. Support yourself spiritually through prayers and listening to words of encouragement and inspiration.

# Chapter Thirteen:
## Releasing Negative Emotions

Releasing negative emotions can be difficult. When you have tried everything and nothing has worked, the methods described in this chapter may help. These methods are for those people who do not like sharing their bad experiences or hurt with others, and may be their best choice. These methods worked for me and are still working. They might look simple and seem insignificant until you try them and then realize they work.

*Take the Gratitude Journey*
On May 3, 2016, I got an email invitation from Tom Ziglar. He said that he would like to invite me on a journey with him. He then gave me a quote from his dad, Zig Ziglar. Hilary Hinton "Zig" Ziglar (November 6, 1926– November 28, 2012) was an American author, salesman, and motivational speaker. The quote reads: Gratitude is the healthiest of all human emotions. The more you express gratitude for what you have, the more likely you will have even more to express gratitude for.

He then described the journey:
"Research done by Phillippa Lally and released in the European Journal of Social Psychology indicates that it takes 66 days to form a new habit. I don't know about you, but if gratitude is the healthiest of all human emotions, and the more grateful we are, the more we must be grateful for, then I say let's make a gratitude a habit! Join me.

"Here is the gratitude journey we can do together. Each day write down three things you are grateful for on a list. You can keep a journal, put it in your Smartphone, send yourself an email, whatever you like. Each day the three things you write down must be different than the previous days'—you can write something on the list only one time! Each day review your list and add three new things. We will do this together for 66 days—the time it takes to make gratitude a habit. At the end of 66 days we will have 198 things we are grateful for, and our minds will constantly be looking for new things to be grateful for."

The journey of gratitude is my recommendation for developing the skills for emotional release. This is because it is a conscious act and a choice for those who desire to have healthy emotions. When Tom sent me this email, I was happy to be part of the group of people who would be exploring the healthy benefits of living a grateful life. It is a rare and profitable journey. Only a few can dive into it, and only a handful can complete it.

Complaining is common. Everyone you meet has something to complain about. We complain about our spouse, children, parents, work, church, friends, colleagues, neighbours, business, and even material stuff like our shoes, clothes, car, house, and so on. It is often the bad experience that is shared. We rarely share good news. This is because we think we are better off doing so. But that is not true. Complaining does not help our emotions. It does not solve the problem we are facing. It only informs people about our problem so that they can empathize with us.

The attitude of gratitude is the greatest thing to have. Grateful people are joyful, hopeful, and successful. Success does not come to the grumpy and angry. Success is attracted by people who love people, who do their work cheerfully, and who have no room for aggression. These negative vices bring unhealthy lifestyles, which deter success. Start the gratitude journey today. Do it to release negative emotions, heal your soul, and restore your life.

*Release Through Giving*
Giving could be the least thing anyone might want to do when it comes to releasing emotions. Giving is a thing of the heart and the top skill anyone can develop. Giving when you think you should not give is an effective way of dealing with hostile behaviour.

I have seen people become humbled by the act of giving. The effect of giving is bi-directional. It affects the receiver as well as the giver. This is because giving touches the heart. The impact can go beyond a refusal to accept what is being offered. That is how powerful giving can be. When you give a worker (especially one who has harassed you in the past) a hand to move his car that is stuck in the snow, it will touch his inner being and cause him to rethink his attitude toward you.

It pays to be nice. It pays to give. As the old saying goes, "Givers never lack." It's like a seed that will grow and bear fruit. There is always something in return for anything that one gives. The return might take time and may not be immediate like a seed or an investment.

I once offered help to a colleague who had been hostile to me at work. He refused because he was angry and did not want to have a conversation with me. The following day, he was having trouble with his machine, and I came by again for the same reason. He accepted my help because he was desperately needing my help at that point. A few minutes later, we resumed our usual conversation. All misunderstanding had vanished, and friendliness was restored, just by lending a helping hand.

*Release through Music*
James Clear shared the story of David Binanay on his website in a blog post entitled "Mozart as Medicine: The Health Benefits of Music." This is a story of healing through music. Here is how the story was narrated by Clear: David Binanay started playing the violin when he was five. By age twelve, he performed at the world-famous Carnegie Hall in New York City and, soon after, at the White House.

In 2006, fresh off graduation from Villanova University, Binanay was positioned perfectly to build his life around music. He had just moved into his own place and started a job at a high-end violin shop.
That's when he noticed the bleeding. It was a gastrointestinal bleed. Binanay had experienced one before, and he called his mom to let her know what was happening. She wanted to help, but David stopped her. "Don't worry about it. I'm going to handle it myself," he said.

This was the first time Binanay tried to handle a serious health issue on his own. When he arrived at the hospital, things began to spiral out of control. His hands started shaking and his mind began to separate from reality. "It was my first psychotic episode," David recalls.

The situation went downhill fast. After resolving the bleeding issue and leaving the hospital, Binanay's psychosis continued. He started having delusions and became fearful of everything. "I couldn't even walk into a grocery store because of the fear," he says. "I didn't really know what I was afraid of, but I feared for my life. In the span of one week, I went from being normal to having a complete psychotic breakdown."

This was the peak of David's psychosis, but his battle was just beginning. He would struggle with schizophrenia for the next five years. His medications worked, but David had trouble sticking to them. There was one thing, however, that always seemed to help.

"My dad would look at me and say, 'Dave, go get your violin.'"
Music stopped the pain. "Every time I played, I noticed a change," David said. "I would channel my emotions through my music. The fear would turn to music. It would turn to sound."

A new medication schedule helped too. David found it much easier to stick to his medication when he switched from pills to injections, which he only needed once a month.

Today, after a five-year battle, Binanay has made a full recovery. He plays his violin up to 10 hours every day and runs a non-profit, Music Over Mind, that performs free music shows at hospitals for people suffering from mental illness. "Music has been my catalyst for recovery," Binanay says. "It has been a 180-degree turnaround. From complete loss to total re-birth. I recently got married. I have my own place with my wife. I feel like I'm a better person than before my illness."

Music is a form of entertainment that puts sounds together in a way that people like or find interesting, inspiring, or informative. Aside from the entertainment aspect of music, music can soothe pain, release hurtful feelings, and ultimately bring healing to the soul.

Hundreds of studies have been conducted by researchers on the effects of music on the mind and emotions. The studies have proven the therapeutic benefits of music, including transforming the mind, changing mood, slowing heart rate, and giving respite. There is healing power in music that brings peace to your heart.

One thing about music is that it serves different purposes. This is why there are different types of music: jazz, blues, country, bluegrass, rock, dance, gospel, and so on. Classical music is a conventional form of music following long- established principles, unlike forms such as folk, jazz, or popular tradition.

The type of music you listen to determines the result you will have in your life. There is music that inspires hatred and encourages hostility and aggression. Calm music touches the human soul in a different way than does rock music. Listening to music makes me feel good when my heart is troubled. My choice of music for release of emotion is hymns, classical, or gospel. I also sing to release emotion. It is an effective and great way to tell your raging emotions to calm down. Singing is the act of expression that presses upon your heart and thoughts the very experience that you want to have. If I want to have peace, I say sing a peaceful song.

My favourite songs are songs of gratitude. This is because gratitude has a way of uplifting the soul. It brings hope. It gives me a sense of worth. It makes me realize that all I am and all I have is a gift. In spite of the trouble in your life, there is something to be grateful for. One of my favourite songs of gratitude is "10,000 Reasons" by Matt Redman. I also sing songs that soothes me in times of trouble. One of the songs is "It Is Well with My Soul," which is a hymn written by Horatio Spafford in 1876. This hymn was written after traumatic events in Spafford's life, including the death of his son at the age of two, the 1871 Great Chicago Fire that ruined his finances, and a shipwreck that claimed all four of Spafford's daughters. His wife, Anna, was the only one who survived. "It Is Well with My Soul" and "Peace" by Lionel Peterson bring great relief to my soul when I am overwhelmed and confused. Hillsong Worship songs bring me to the point of relaxation and reflection. They uplift and transform me inwardly. They restore my joy and refresh me.

In order to move towards forgiveness, I listen to the Hezekiah song track titled, "I Need You to Survive." It is usually difficult to ignore those who hurt you, especially when you run into them frequently at work or social meetings. I listen to this song to condition both my mind and emotions to embrace love for everyone. This song reminds me that we need each other irrespective of our individual flaws and shortcomings. It is a song that expresses love, welcomes love, and promises love. It gives emotional support and encouragement.

*Release through Prayer*
On June 25, 2016, Tom Ziglar at Ziglar Inc. sent me an email that was titled "The Secret of Handling Pressure." The email began with the question, "Are you under pressure?" and continued to ask, "Have you ever felt like just 'one more thing' on the top of what you are dealing with will put you over the edge?"

He continued by quoting Bryan Flanagan, one of the top Ziglar sales trainers, who said, "Process takes pressure off the person." Then he added, "When you create processes and systems to handle your personal and business life, pressure no longer builds up—it moves on through as energy, helping you to move forward rather than as a weight that crushes you."

Tom Ziglar shared this most important truth that we all often ignore when dealing with life issues. He said that he has a process that takes pressure off every area of his life. He called this process "2 Chairs." He explains "2 Chairs" this way: "Every day I get up early and have one-on-one time with God. He takes one chair; I take the other. I share my burdens with Him and then I listen … This process releases my pressure." In conclusion, he then said to me, "Feeling pressure? 2 Chairs!"

"2 Chairs" was what I learned from my parents. My mom would

always ask me if I had prayed about my problem. As a kid, it didn't make sense to talk to an invisible Being about what I felt mentally, emotionally, and physically. But I did pray anyway. Prayer was just a sort of thing that I had to do. When I became more mature, it dawned on me that there is some kind of release that happens after praying.

I decided to find out if prayers worked. I remember as a teenager having a boil on my left hand, and I was worried that my classmates at school were going to laugh and make fun of me the next day. I then remembered that I could share my concerns with God, who would understand my feelings better than anyone else. I prayed and went to bed. The following day, the boil was gone.

The source of my worry was taken care of when I shared it with God. Now as an adult, I could resort to medication for a minor ailment. But I don't know if a medication could cure within twenty-four hours. Perhaps it could. A "miracle" is the name given to an event that is beyond the natural. Only the supernatural can perform it.

I have had many painful emotional experiences, some of which have been resolved by sharing my feelings with a trusted friend. But there have been tough times in my life when words of encouragement were meaningless. The encourager would think I was listening and probably feeling better, but instead the sympathetic words were adding to the injury. This was the case when I lost my dad in 2004 and my mom in 2011. Many sympathizers came with kind words to make me feel better, but their words didn't help.

When you cannot trust anyone with what you are going through, you can trust God with it through prayers. Even if you don't believe in God, it doesn't stop you from giving it a try. When you try it, you will see that it works. Prayer releases emotion. Prayer is a spiritual exercise and medium through which pressure, pains, hurt, and worry can be expressed and released.

When forgiveness is tough, prayer makes it easy. People who often pray rarely go to bed with anger or wake up with it. They release their hurtful feelings during prayer, and relief comes from God. When Stephen was dragged out of the city and stoned to death, he knelt and shouted, "Lord, don't blame them for what they have done." Then, he died. Before Jesus was crucified on the cross, Pilate gave orders for him to be beaten with a whip. The soldier made a crown out of thorn branches and put it on him. He was taken away and was nailed to the cross. While on the cross before His death, Jesus said, "Father, forgive these people! They don't know what they are doing."

Life is beautiful when we give room for forgiveness. It is too short to hold onto anger and bitterness. It favours everyone when we nourish love and protect the peace of our relationship with each other. We will enjoy peace and the joy of beautiful relationships with people in our home, workplace, and the community at large when we accept that we are human, and we are not perfect.

It is important to accept our offender's apology and forgive them even when they refuse to admit they were wrong. Also, it is important for us to say "sorry" when we hurt other people's feelings. When we say "sorry," it means we love and care about other people's feelings, especially the feelings of the person to whom we are apologizing. "I am sorry" is not a sign of weakness. It is the way we express that we acknowledge our human limitations—the imperfection that exists in every human being.

Everyone makes mistakes, and there are no exemptions. Regardless of one's status in society, mistakes are common to all men. The only difference is that it is only the strong and wise people who admit they are wrong and say "sorry." The strong and the wise create enough room in their heart to forgive other people when they offend them. It becomes difficult to have a beautiful and happy life where ego and ignorance reigns. It becomes difficult to tolerate and work with other people.

The ignorance and unbalanced perception that blindside and influence our words and actions often creates enormous opportunities for increasing tensions and misunderstanding. When we ignore the convictions of our heart to apologize or forgive, we are clouded emotionally as well as mentally with feelings and thoughts. Sometimes we opt for silence, and prolonged silence may not be helpful. Prolonged silence in the presence of strong and persisting heartfelt conviction can affect our emotional state and may lead to self-imprisonment.

When we admit we are wrong and say sorry, it is like medicine for us. It heals our relationships and opens room for more conversation and understanding, while strengthening the bond we have together. Peace and unity prevail over the hurts, and the tension becomes non-existent. As this becomes the case, our relationship with one another progresses and grows deeper in understanding and commitment.

Rendering an apology is a brave thing to do. It might sound foolish to some, but it is only the brave that acknowledges their mistakes and say sorry. Have you ever compared how it feels when you apologize and when you walk away in pride? The difference is the refreshing experience that comes with apology and the reconciliation that follows. The commitment to the union is kept, and the relationship grows and becomes stronger.

Prayer helps forgiveness happen in fullness. Grudges, malice, and harmful intention cannot withstand the power of effective prayer. It brings spiritual refreshment that can heal our hurt feelings.

# Taking Stock of Your Emotional Health

When do people go to the hospital? They go to the hospital when they are sick. The problem with waiting until you are sick before you visit the hospital is that it can cost you more than it does to regularly check your health status. People who monitor their health status rarely call in sick or get hospitalized. This is because they take care of the microorganism that causes disease before they succumb to it. This applies to your emotional health. If you monitor the temperature of your emotions and listen to the heartbeat of your feelings, you can maintain a realistic emotional calmness and stability.

If possible, I recommend that you take out your daily schedule just before bedtime and examine your emotions. Try to make it a daily habit, because to carry negative emotions through the night can ruin the next day. Actually, anger should be managed before sunset. Going to bed with anger and other negative emotions can make you lose sleep and affect your health.

GRADING METHOD
Personal Information: Score your personal information section first. It consists of ten questions about your profile. The answers to these questions reveal your least changing status; for example, if you have a family of seven, that will not change until kids become adults and move out the house. The highest score to the questions on personal information section is thirty. Score each line and add up your score. Subtract what you get from the maximum score to get the estimated value of your emotional state.

General Information: When scoring your general information, make sure you read thoroughly and answer with clarity. Please do not try to be nice to yourself by choosing a lesser value score. When you are done, add up your scores. Subtract what you get from the maximum score to get the estimated value of your emotional state. General information questions reflect aspects of your health with greater chances of improvement. Work on improving those aspects as you can. Maintaining lower than the average should be your goal. Always remember that you can take charge of your life and control many of the things that you experience. If there are some things you cannot control, you can choose to control how they influence you.

Please take the exercise that is appropriate for you. This survey is divided into three exercises for three categories of people—students, workers, and the retired (aged).

EXERCISE 1 is strictly for students—those who are in school (and who may or may not have a part-time job). If you are taking courses that prevent you from having a full-time job, you belong to this category.

EXERCISE 2 is strictly for full-time workers—those who spend about forty hours of their week working in an office, factory, or business. If you aren't in an academic program, and are employed or looking for a job, you belong to this category.

EXERCISE 3 is strictly for the retiree or senior—who are enrolled in any pension plan. It is also for those who have retired early, including those who have injuries that prevent them from returning to work.

EXERCISE 1
(For working and studying students only)
Academic Performance and General Information
The following exercise will give you an idea of how despondent you are. It addresses relevant facts that will help in self-examination. Circle or write out the number you feel corresponds to your viewpoint and add them up. The results may motivate you to seek out help if needed. Please complete this exercise on your own. When you have finished, total the number you entered in the provided spaces.
[30 Marks max]

Marital Status
Single (dependent) .....................................................0
Married (both working) .............................................1
Separated/divorced (with kid[s]) ...................................2
Widowed (with kid[s]) ...............................................3

Who pays the bill or fees (both home and school)?
Parents/guardians      0      Husband/wife      1
Shared (among family/roommates)              2
Self (all alone)                                3

Size of household
(number of people who live in your house, including yourself)
Alone (with good income)                      0
Two                                           1
Three                                         2
More than three                               3
Academic status

Online (at your pace)                         0
Full time (high and tertiary school)          1
Part time (post-graduate school)              2
Part time (concurrent program)                3

Travel time to school
Online                                    0
Drive/bus fifteen minutes                 1
Drive/bus thirty minutes                  2
Drive/bus more than thirty minutes        3

Other source of income (if any)
Residual income                           0
Part-time job                             1
Loan                                      2
None                                      3

Family history of depression or mental illness
Never                                     0
Rarely                                    1
Often                                     2
Always                                    3

Childhood and upbringing experience
Single or both parents/guardians (caring)   0
Single or both parents/guardians (strict)   1
Strict and severe parents                 2
Social isolation                          3

Traumatic experience
None                                      0
Family violence                           1
Bereavement                               2
Abuse/Neglect                             3

Economic status
Affluent                                  0

Average                                  1
Below average                            2
Poor                                     3


[75 Marks max]

**0. Never    1. Rarely    2. Often    3. Always**

Rate the following based on the past year in school.
I have been bullied, threatened, or harassed by a schoolmate. [ ]
I have felt that I am doing badly at school
(based on my performance). [ ]
I find it difficult to associate with my schoolmates. [ ]
I ask questions about things I do not understand. [ ]
I have been absent from school without a genuine reason. [ ]
I have been discouraged about doing my homework. [ ]
I have worried about past academic failure. [ ]
I have considered dropping out of school or quitting my job. [ ]

Rate the following based on your feelings about your school system over the past three months.
I have a constant feeling of sadness, anxiety,
and emptiness every day. [ ]
I am stressed, frustrated, and not coping. [ ]
I have poor self-esteem and am not able to talk
to teachers or schoolmates. [ ]
I feel hated, ignored, unimportant, and unaccepted. [ ]
Rate the following based on the past three months.
I have lost interest in my hobbies. [ ]
I sleep too much or too little. [ ]
I have lost or gained weight without trying. [ ]
I feel tired/lacking in energy. [ ]
Rate the following based on the past three months.

I lack concentration.                                    [ ]
I think in slow or fast motion.                          [ ]
I keep forgetting things.                                [ ]
I have trouble making decisions.                         [ ]
I wish to take my own life.                              [ ]
Rate the following based on the past three weeks.
I avoid friends and relations.                           [ ]
I self-manage my symptoms with alcohol or drugs.         [ ]
I have anxiety, bitterness, and/or nightmares.           [ ]
I having aches and pains without an obvious cause.       [ ]

Result of Taking Stock of Your Mental Health: . . . . . . . . . . . . . . . . .%

MAKE YOUR DECISION

Carefully consider your scores in the above self-evaluation exercise. From your grading and scoring, determine if your self-evaluation is great or poor. Then, consider what you want to do about your emotional wellbeing and make a decision on how you can improve your emotional status through the knowledge you have gained through descriptions and examples outlined in this book. Write down your decision in the space(s) provided below (for examples: Yes or No) and ensure you follow through.

Seek help through.

———————————————————————

Build/rebuild my relationships.

———————————————————————

Resolve conflict or misunderstanding.

———————————————————————

Choose to forgive and let go.

| Exercise |
|---|
| Prioritize my tasks. |
| Deepen my understanding in dealing with people. |
| Stay away from negative people and things. |
| Take interest in the things I love. |
| Make friends with people that share the same vision or dream. |

EXERCISE 2
(For full-time working people)
The following exercise will help give you an idea of how despondent you are. It addresses relevant facts that will help in self-examination. Circle or write out the number you feel corresponds to your viewpoint and add up your score. Your results may motivate you to seek help if needed. Please complete this exercise on your own. When you have finished, total the number you entered in the provided spaces.
[30 Marks max]
Marital Status

| | |
|---|---|
| Single (dependent) | 0 |
| Married (both working) | 1 |
| Separated/divorced (with kid[s]) | 2 |
| Widowed (with kid[s]) | 3 |

Who pays the bill?
| | |
|---|---|
| Parents/guardians | 0 |
| Husband/wife | 1 |
| Shared (among family/roommates) | 2 |
| Self (all alone) | 3 |

Size of household (number of people who live in your house, including yourself)
| | |
|---|---|
| Alone (with good income) | 0 |
| Two | 1 |
| Three | 2 |
| More than three | 3 |

Type of job or employment
| | |
|---|---|
| Private Service (well paid) | 0 |
| Public Service (well paid) | 1 |
| Business (shared duties) | 2 |
| Self-employed (all alone) | 3 |

Travel time to school
| | |
|---|---|
| Online | 0 |
| Drive/bus fifteen minutes | 1 |
| Drive/bus thirty minutes | 2 |
| Drive/Bus more than thirty minutes | 3 |

Other source of income (if any)
| | |
|---|---|
| Residual income | 0 |
| Part-time job | 1 |

| | |
|---|---|
| Loan | 2 |
| None | 3 |

Family history of depression or mental illness
| | |
|---|---|
| Never | 0 |
| Rarely | 1 |
| Often | 2 |
| Always | 3 |

Childhood and upbringing experience
| | |
|---|---|
| Single or both parents/guardians (caring) | 0 |
| Single or both parents/guardians (strict) | 1 |
| Strict and severe | 2 |
| Social isolation | 3 |

Traumatic experience
| | |
|---|---|
| None | 0 |
| Family violence | 1 |
| Bereavement | 2 |
| Abuse/neglect | 3 |

Economic status
| | |
|---|---|
| Affluent | 0 |
| Average | 1 |
| Below average | 2 |
| Poor | 3 |

[75 Marks max.]

**0. Never    1. Rarely    2. Often    3. Always**

Work Experience and Other Information
Rate the following based on the past one to two years.
I have been laid off, fired, or have quit my job.                    [ ]

Based on my performance, I feel I am doing badly at work. [ ]
I have failed to meet a deadline without a genuine reason. [ ]
I have been absent from work without a genuine reason? [ ]
I have been advised, warned, or confronted about
my poor performance. [ ]
I have been worried and considered quitting my job. [ ]
Rate the following based on the past three months.
I have lost interest in my work and hobbies
(e.g. cooking or sports). [ ]
I sleep too much or too little. [ ]
I am always sad. [ ]
I have lost or gained weight. [ ]
I feeling tired/lacking in energy [ ]
I have no appetite for food or interest in sex (one or both). [ ]
Rate your thinking based on the past three months.
I lack concentration. [ ]
I think in slow or fast motion. [ ]
I keep forgetting things. [ ]
I have trouble making decisions. [ ]
I wish I was dead. [ ]
Rate your day-to-day behaviours based on the past three weeks.
I avoid fellow workers, friends, and relations. [ ]
I self-manage my symptoms with alcohol or drugs. [ ]
I have aches and pains without an obvious cause. [ ]

**0. Strongly disagree  1. Disagree    2. Agree    3. Strongly agree**

How would you describe your income, responsibilities at work, and workplace conditions?
Low income [ ]
Physically demanding [ ]
Stressful, frustrating and difficult to cope with [ ]
Increasing work demands without increase in wages or salary [ ]
Slow and planning to downsize [ ]

Result of Taking Stock of Your Mental Health: . . . . . . . . . . . . . . . . .%

## MAKE YOUR DECISION

Carefully consider your scores in the above self-evaluation exercise. From your grading and scoring, determine if your self-evaluation is great or poor. Then, consider what you want to do about your emotional wellbeing and make a decision on how you can improve your emotional status through the knowledge you have gained through descriptions and examples outlined in this book. Write down your decision in the space(s) provided below (for examples: Yes or No) and ensure you follow through.

Seek help through

---

Build/rebuild my relationship

---

Resolve conflict or misunderstanding

---

Choose to forgive and let go

---

Exercise

---

Prioritize my tasks

---

Deepen my understanding in dealing with people

| |
|---|
| Stay away from negative people and things |

| |
|---|
| Take an interest in the things I love |

| |
|---|
| Make friends with people that share the same vision or dream |

EXERCISE 3
(For Retiree or Senior)
The following exercise will give you an idea of how despondent you are. It addresses relevant facts that will help in self-examination. Circle or write out the number you feel corresponds to your viewpoint and add them up. Your results may motivate you to seek out help if needed. Please complete this exercise on your own. When you have finished, total the number you entered in the provided spaces.

[30 Marks max.]
Marital Status
| | |
|---|---|
| Single (dependent) | 0 |
| Married | 1 |
| Separated/divorced (with kid[s]) | 2 |
| Widowed (with kid[s]) | 3 |

Who pays the bill or fees?
| | |
|---|---|
| Husband/wife | 1 |
| Shared (among family/roommates) | 2 |
| Self (all alone) | 3 |

Size of household (number of people who live in your house, including yourself)?
| | |
|---|---|
| Alone (with good income) | 0 |
| Two | 1 |
| Three | 2 |
| More than three | 3 |

Family History of depression or mental illness
| | |
|---|---|
| Never | 0 |
| Rarely | 1 |
| Often | 2 |
| Always | 3 |

Childhood and upbringing experience
| | |
|---|---|
| Single or both parents/guardians (caring) | 0 |
| Single or both parents/guardians (strict) | 1 |
| Strict and severe | 2 |
| Social isolation | 3 |

Traumatic experience
| | |
|---|---|
| None | 0 |
| Family violence | 1 |
| Bereavement | 2 |
| Abuse/neglect | 3 |

Economic status
| | |
|---|---|
| Affluent | 0 |
| Average | 1 |
| Below average | 2 |
| Poor | 3 |

Type of retirement and/or the reason for retirement
| | |
|---|---|
| Early retirement | 0 |

Retirement age 1
Workplace injury 2
Accident victim 3

Type of health status
Healthy 0
Less-coordination illness 1
Mental illness 2
Terminal illness 3

Type of caregiving environment
At own home/senior housing with family
or caregiver 1
At home with family visiting occasionally 2
At home alone 3

[75 Marks max]

| 0. Never | 1. Rarely | 2. Often | 3. Always |
|---|---|---|---|

After Work Experience and Other Information
Rate the following based on the past one to two years.
I have people living with me who love and care for me. [ ]
I have people I can easily and freely talk to about anything. [ ]
I indulge in alcohol or drugs. [ ]
I have been worried about my present and future. [ ]
Rate the following based on the past three months.
I have lost interest in my hobbies (e.g. cooking or watching sports). [ ]
I sleep too much or too little. [ ]
I have lost or gained weight without trying. [ ]
I feel tired/lacking in energy. [ ]
Rate your thinking based on the past three months.
I lack concentration. [ ]

I think in slow or fast motion. [ ]
I keep forgetting things. [ ]
I have trouble making decisions. [ ]
I wish I was dead. [ ]
Rate your day-to-day feelings based on the past three weeks.
I am not getting on with family or friends. [ ]
I self-manage my symptoms with alcohol or drugs. [ ]
I have anxiety, bitterness, and/or nightmares [ ]
I have aches and pains without an obvious cause. [ ]
I put myself down and/or feel worthless. [ ]
I feel lonely or abandoned. [ ]

0. Strongly disagree 1. Disagree  2. Agree  3. Strongly agree

How would you describe your living and financial condition?
Low pension [ ]
No other source of income [ ]
Too expensive to handle [ ]
Large debt [ ]
Support of family member or friend [ ]
No social support (e.g. religion, club, or group) [ ]
Result of Taking Stock of Your Mental Health: ................
.%


YOUR DECISION

Carefully consider your scores in the above self-evaluation exercise. From your grading and scoring, determine if your self-evaluation is great or poor. Then, consider what you want to do about your emotional wellbeing and make a decision on how you can improve your emotional status through the knowledge you have gained through descriptions and examples outlined in this book. Write down your decision in the space(s) provided below (for examples: Yes or No) and ensure you follow through.

Seek help through

..........................................

Build/rebuild my relationships

..........................................

Resolve conflict or misunderstanding

..........................................

Choose to forgive and let go

..........................................

Exercise

..........................................

Prioritize my tasks

..........................................

Deepen my understanding in dealing with people

..........................................

Stay away from negative people and things

..........................................

Take an interest in the things I love

..........................................

Make friends with people that share the same vision or dream

..........................................

# Bibliography

*2014 Isla Vista Killing.* (2014, May 23). Retrieved from Wikipedia: https://en.wikipedia.org/wwiki/2014_Isla_Vista_killings

American Psychiatric. (June 2000, June 2000). *Diagnostic and Statistical Manual of Mental Disorders.* Wwashinngton DC: American Psychiatric Publishing.

American Society for the Positive Care of Children. (2017). *Bullying Statistics and Information.* Retrieved from American SPCC: http://www.americanspcc.org/bullying/statistics-and-information/

*Arrested Development.* (Accessed 2019). Retrieved from Wikipedia: https://en.wikipedia.org/wiki/Arrested_development#cite_note-4

Ayler, A. (Accessed 2017). *Albert Ayler.* Retrieved from Wikipedia.org: https://en.wikipedia.org/wiki/Albert_Ayler

*Bipolar Depression: Highlights of the First International Connference on Bipolar Disorder.* (1994, June 23). Retrieved from Mental Health: https://www..mentalhealth.com/mag1/p51-bpcf.html

Bright, M. (2006, July 3). *Mary Maria - Mary Parks - Albert Ayler.* Retrieved from Organissimo: http://www.organissimo,org/forum/index.php?/topic/28100-mary-maria-parks-albert-ayler

*Cain and Abel.* (Accessed 2017). Retrieved from Wikipedia.org: https://en.wikipedia.org/wiki/Cain_and_Abel

Cameron, G. (2014, December 2). *Congressional aide resigns after slamming Obama daughters.* . Retrieved from Reuters: https://www.reuters.com/article/us-usa-obama-daughters/congressional-aide-resignns-after-slamming-obama-daughters-idUSKCNN0JG1NNX20141202

*Charles F. Kettering.* (Accessed 2017). Retrieved from https:en.wikipedia.org/wiki/Charles_F._Kettering

Clear, J. (Accessed 2017). *The Health Benefits of Music.* Retrieved from James Clear: http://www.jamesclear.com/music-therapy

CNN. (2013, July 2). *Enron Fast Facts.* Retrieved from CNN:

http://www.cnn.com/2013/07/02/us/enron-fast-facts/index.html

Dow, I. (2014, October 3). *Bullying Statistics*. Retrieved from No Bullying: http://nobullying.com/bullying-statistics-2014/

*Edward Howard Armstrong*. (Accessed 2017). Retrieved from Wikipedia: https://www.en.wikipedia.org/wiki/Edward_Howard_Armstrong

Ellesse. (2017, June 4). *66 Famous failures of people who never give up*. Retrieved from Goal Setting College: http://www.goal=setting--college.com/inspiration/famous-failures/

Elyse, W. (2017, January 10). *Man Fired for attending Son'sBirth is Flooded with Job Offers*. Retrieved from HuffPost: https://www.huffpost.com/entry/dadd-fired-birth-son-job-offers_n_586ff2a1e4b099cdb0fd1892

*Eron Scandal*. (Accessed 2017). Retrieved from Wikipedia: https://www.en.wikipedia.org/wiki/Eron_Scandal

Famous Scientists. (2014, October 27). *John Dalton*. Retrieved from Famous Scientists: http://www.famousscientists.org/john-dalton

Farberov, S. (2016, October 19). *'I'm the victim': Former teacher, 24, who slept hundreds of times with 17-year-old student claims he ruined her life after sharing her naked selfies with friends and she was forced to become a STRIPPER*. Retrieved from Daily Mail: https://www.dailymail.co.uk/news/article-3852630/Former-teacher-24-slept-hundreds-times-17-year-old-student-claims-ruined-life-sharing-naked-selfies-friends-forced-STRIPPER.html

*Francois de La Rochefoucauld*. (Accessed 2017). Retrieved from Wikipedia: https://www.en.eikipedia.org/wiki/Francois_de_La_Rochefoucauld

Galen, E. (2012, January 15). *Man Jailed for Chainsaw Road Rage*. Retrieved from Toronto Sun: http://www.torontosun.com/2012/01/15/man-jailed-for-chainsaw-road-rage

*George Sanders*. (Accessed 2017). Retrieved from Wikipedia:

https://www.wikipedia.org/wiki/George_Sanders

Greg, A. (2014, May 24). *'I will slaughter every single blonde s\*\*t I see: lonely killer posted chilling video warning of 'retribution' because he was still a virgin at age 22'.* Retrieved from Daily Mail: http://www.dailymail.co.uk/news/article-2638049/7-dead-drive-shooting-near-UC-Santa-Babara.htm

*Hans Langsdorff.* (Accessed 2017). Retrieved from Wikipedia: https://www.en.wikipedia.org/wiki/Hans_Langsdorff

Hasselbring, B. (1969, December 31). *The Chemical Connection to Depression.* Retrieved from HowStuffWorks: https://health.howstuffworks.com/mental-health/depression/facts/the-chemical-connection-to-depression.htm

*Hatred.* (Accessed 2017). Retrieved from The Free Dictionary: http://www.thefreedictionary.com/hatred

*Havelock Ellis.* (Accessed 2017). Retrieved from Wikipedia: https://www.en.wikipedia.org/wiki/Havelock_Ellis

*J. Clifford Baxter.* (Accessed 2017). Retrieved from Wikipedia: https://www.en.wikipedia.org/J._Clifford_Baxter

Jake. (2009, May 26). *Pamela Rogers Turner.* Retrieved from Zimbio: http://www.zimbio.com/Pamela+Rogers+Turner/articles/zTQENnMYVVc/4+Pamela+Rogers+Turner

Jake. (2009, May 26). *Pamela Smart.* Retrieved from Zimbio: http://www.zimbio.com/Pamela+Smart/articles/QDui7KGVuuX/5+Pamela+Smart

*Jason Altom.* (Accessed 2017). Retrieved from Wikipedia: https://www.en.wikipedia.org/wiki/Jason_Altom

*Jean-Baptiste Lamarck.* (Accessed 2017). Retrieved from Wikipedia: https://en.wikipedia.org/wiki/Jean-Baptiste_Lamarck

*John 3:16 (KJV).* (Accessed 2017). Retrieved from Bible Gateway: https://www..biblegateway.com/passage/?search=John+3%3A16&version=KJV

Kate, A. (2005, September 4). *An Excruciating Excess of Reality.* Retrieved from The New York Times: http://www.nytimes.com/2005/09/04/arts/television/an-excruciating-excess-of-reality.html

*Laozi.* (Accessed 2017). Retrieved from Wikipedia:

https://www.en.wikipedia.org/laozi

*Luke 6:38 (KJV)*. (Accessed 2017). Retrieved from Bible Gateway: http://www.biblegateway.com/passage/?search=Luke+6%3A38&version=KJV

*Max Scheler*. (Accessed 2017). Retrieved from Wikipedia: http://www.en.wikipedia.com/Max_Scheler

Max, S. (1973). *Formalism in Ethics and Non-formal Ethics of Values: A new attempt toward the foundation of an ethical personalism.* Northern Universy Press.

McCarty, J. F. (2007, May 13). *Strongsville ex-teacher pleads guilty.* Retrieved from Free Republic: http://www.freerepublic.com/focus/f-news/1849401/posts

*Milan*. (Accessed 2017). Retrieved from Wikipedia: https://www.en.wikipedia.org/wiki/Milan_Babic

Phillip W. Long, M. (1994, June 23). *Bipolar Depression: Highlights of the First International Conference on Bipolar Disorder.* Retrieved from Mental Health: https://www.mentalhealth.com/mag1/p51-bpcf.html

*Preventing Suicide: A global imperative.* (2014, August 17). Retrieved from World Health Organization: https://who.int/publications-detail/preventing-suicide-a-global-imperative

*Psychomotor Retardation.* (2014, February 10). Retrieved from Wikipedia: https://www.en.wikipedia.org/Psychomotor_Retardation

*Ralph Barton*. (Accessed 2017). Retrieved from Wikipedia: https://www.en.wikipedia.org/wiki/Ralph_Barton

Reporter, D. M. (2013, December 12). *Chanel's Dallas show branded 'an offensive mockery' by Native Americans over 'sacred' feathered headdresses.* Retrieved from Daily Mail: http://www.dailymail.co.uk/femail/article-2522291/Chanels-Dallas-branded-offensive-mockery-Native-Americans-sacred-feathered-headdresses.html

*Romans 12:21*. (Accessed 2017). Retrieved from Bible Gateway: https://www.biblegateway.com/passage/?search=Romans+12&versionn=NIV

Rose, R. (2015, December 21). *See the awkward moment when Steve Harvey Announce the wrong miss universe* . Retrieved from

Cosmopolitan: http://www.cosmopolitan.com/entertainment/news/a51084/miss-universe-wrong-winner-announced

Sarah, L. (2014, July 16). *'I'm yours forever': Two years in prison for Calgary teacher, 30, caught having sex with boy, 16.* Retrieved from National Post: https://nationalpost.com/news/canada/im-yours-forever-two-years-in-prison-for-calgary-teacher-30-caught-having-sex-with-boy-16

Sarah, L. (2014, September 19). *It Wasn't Relativity that Won Einstein His Nobel Prize.* Retrieved from The Atlantic:: https://www.theatlantic.com/technology/archives/20/14/09/einstein-didn't-win--a-nobel-for-relativity-he-was-on-it-for-this/380541

*Stuart Adamson.* (Accessed 2017). Retrieved from Wikipedia: http://www.en.wiki/stuart_Adamson

Stuart, C. (2012, October 8). *Why Einstein never received a Nobel prize for relativity.* Retrieved from The Guardian: http://www.theguardian.com/science/across-the-universe/2012/oct/08/einstein-nobel-prize--relativity

The New York Times. (1989, July 23). *Forrest Anderson, Ex-Governor oof Montana Kills Himself at 76.* Retrieved from The New York Times: http://www.nytimes.com/1989/07/23/obituaries/forrest-anderson-ex-governor-of-montana-kills-himself-at-76.html

Toumit, V. (2017, February 7). *This is my last share for linkedin.* Retrieved from LinkedIn: https://www.linkedin.com/pulse/success-linkedin-victoria-toumit

*Whistleblower Protection Act of 1989.* (2020, July). Retrieved from CONGRESS.GOV: https://www.congress.gov/bill/101st-congress/senate-bill/20/text]

*Whistleblower Protections.* (2020, July). Retrieved from Ontario Securities Comission: https://www.osc.gov.on.ca/en/protections.htm#:~:text=The%20OSC%20will%20make%20all,are%20represented%20by%20a%20lawyer

www.ingramcontent.com/pod-product-compliance
Lightning Source LLC
Chambersburg PA
CBHW030904080526
44589CB00010B/142